ARRIS ILLUSTRATED HISTORIES

ARRIS ILLUSTRATED HISTORIES

LENIN

AND THE RUSSIAN REVOLUTION

ANTONELLA SALOMONI

Translated by David Stryker

ARRIS BOOKS
An imprint of Arris Publishing Ltd
Gloucestershire

First published in Great Britain in 2004 by

Arris Books
An imprint of Arris Publishing Ltd
12 Main Street
Adlestrop
Moreton-in-Marsh
Gloucestershire GL56 0YN
www.arrisbooks.com

This edition of *Lenin and the Russian Revolution* is published by arrangement with
Giunti Editore and Casterman Editions.

ISBN 1 84437 023 2

Printed and bound in Italy

To request our complete catalogue, please call us at **01608 659328**, visit our
web site at: **www.arrisbooks.com**, or e-mail us at: info@arrisbooks.com.

Contents

LENIN AND THE RUSSIAN REVOLUTION

Chapter 1

THE EMPIRE OF THE CZARS

IN 1861, CZAR ALEXANDER II CATAPULTED RUSSIA INTO THE ERA OF REFORMS. BUT THESE WERE INSUFFICIENT TO PREVENT THE CRISIS OF THE IMPERIAL REGIME. IN 1905, THE HUGE EMPIRE WAS IN THE THROES OF ITS FIRST REVOLUTION.

At the beginning of the nineteenth century, Russia was a vast, expanding nation. Over a period of several centuries, the Empire of the Czars reached the Arctic Ocean, the Caspian, and the Baltic, and had conquered all of Siberia, as well as Alaska. A series of victorious wars had led to the annexation of Finland, Poland, and a certain number of territories wrested from Ottoman control. However, Russia's essentially agricultural economy was stuck in another time: there was little urban development and almost no roads to speak of. The immense majority of Russians were concentrated in European Russia, and their status was that of serfs attached to the landed gentry or to the State.

The servitude of the Russian people was one of the pillars of Russian society. According to the 1858 census, there were over 49 million serfs in Russia (22,563,086 belonging to private landowners and 19,370,631 attached to the State). The serfs had two kinds of obligations or duties: a tax in kind (*obrok*) and in labor (*barshchina*). The landowner (*pomeshchik*) enjoyed limitless power over his serfs. He was sole judge of all internal matters except the most serious crimes. He could not impose the death penalty, but he could have someone imprisoned, tortured, or deported to Siberia. Moreover, he had the authority to impose or forbid a marriage, and to sell a portion of his serfs to another landowner. At the end of the eighteenth century one could still see serfs being sold in the market square.

August 1904: Czar Nikolai II blesses a regiment on its way to fight the Japanese. Autocratic rule, still the basis of the Russian state at the beginning of the twentieth century, meant the Czar's total power, total immunity from the law, and a total freedom from accountability toward subjects or popularly elected assemblies. Nikolai II's reactionary domestic policy would foster the growth of the socialist party, the serfs' opposition, and other revolutionary movements. Ph. © L'Illustration/Sygma

The oil rig at Baku was the work of a Swedish chemist, a certain Alfred Nobel (1833–96) who had studied in St. Petersburg. By the end of the nineteenth century, industrialization was in full swing, thanks to French, British, Belgian, and German capital. And society was feeling the disturbing effects of the clash between an ancient agricultural order and the new industrial sector.
Ph © Novosti

The reign of Nikolai I (1825–1855) opened with the repression of the Decabrist insurrection. This uprising, a coalition of officers and liberal aristocrats, sought to introduce a constitutional regime in Russia as well as social reforms. But it led to a brutal counteroffensive against any attempt to question the Czar's absolute power. In 1848, when all of Europe was swept up in republican revolutions, Russian absolutism represented an extreme conservative bastion, giving Russia the well-deserved title of the "Police of Europe."

Sudden defeat in the Crimean War, from 1853–56, was an alarm bell to Alexander II (1855–1881) and to the moderns among the military and political circles of the court, who were well aware of the declining of Russia's economy and social fabric. At any rate, the result of the war pointed out glaring deficiencies in the imperial military, both technologically and in terms of general readiness. Wartime potential could only be achieved by building railroads and creating a steel industry—in other words, by encouraging all-out economic development. But the serfs were constantly on the edge of revolt, and a genuine threat to the regime from the interior took priority. During the Crimean War, a vast insurrection had swept the country, and the people were reminded of the terrible years of Pugachev's revolt (1772–74) that had almost toppled the Czar. The urgency of development and the fear of unrest led Alexander II and the more enlightened sectors of the aristocracy to accelerate reforms deemed indispensable. On March 13, 1876, the Czar pronounced the memorable phrase before the Muscovite nobles: "It is better to abolish serfdom from on high, rather than wait for it to be abolished from below, without our help."

The Age of Reform

After long and protracted preparations, serfdom was formally abolished on February 19, 1861. The serfs recited the Czar's proclamation declaring them "free citizens." This was an historical moment. At least in principle, the serfs suddenly had access to freedoms that the feudal system had denied them for centuries: the right to own personal property, the right to dispose freely of their ability to work, and the right to due process and justice. This was, however, a largely token citizenship. The decision to initiate reform was made more because the Czar wished to maintain Russia's role in the contemporary world, than to foster the creation of a Western-style civil society. Modern

In a factory mess, the workers are squeezed in, with the adults in front and the children in back. At the beginning of the twentieth century, less than ten percent of the population worked in industry. Factories were tied to local supply and demand, and seasonal migration due to agricultural rhythms seriously perturbed production.
Ph © L'Illustration/Sygma

***R**eligious procession in front of the Winter Palace. The Orthodox Church, totally subordinated to the state, contributed to Russia's intellectual stagnation as much as to political despotism. As in other branches of imperial authority, members of the Holy Sinod of Russia were nominated by the Czar; they were the embodiment of his autocratic control over all ecclesiastic affairs.*
Ph © L'Illustration/Sygma

warfare's ever-greater demands on the population were also a major factor. The army was still structured on the feudal system of recruitment, and the recent military debacle cruelly proved the need for the army to have access to each and every citizen. The Czar's dramatic bestowal of equal citizenship for all was primarily for the defense of the Russian State.

It must be said that some segments of the aristocracy were sensitive to liberal ideas and had understood the political values involved in being a player in the global marketplace. They concluded that those in power had to change radically and adopt without hesitation the model of development found in industrialized countries. They would have to renounce a whole series of privileges that were incompatible with a modern society, and whose prolonging would jeopardize Russia's position among the great powers, a position she had occupied—with an historic exception—since Peter the Great (1682–1725).

The abolition of serfdom triggered deep changes in the administration, justice system, schools, and the army. The end of the feudal system meant that the entire legal code had to be adapted to accommodate the equal rights of all citizens before the law, and that new administrative organisms had to be created in the

peripheral areas of the empire. Until then, the chief landowner was also chief justice in all matters pertaining to his serfs, and was the chief administrator in all matters regarding the central authorities. Alexander II initiated a process of reorganizing the judiciary, bringing it to a level more compatible with the rest of Europe, and making local administrative reforms, such as refurbishing the local police apparatus and creating the *zemstvas*, or regional assemblies. These reforms, implemented by 1864, were followed by a similar restructuring of the various sectors of the educational system; some years later, the army was revamped on the Prussian model.

With the advancement of these reforms, however, the era of the aristocracy's dominance was over. The ancient patriarchal relationships were undermined—and an opening was created for the development of a new social class—the bourgeoisie. Although the reforms were primarily in juridical and administrative practices, this essential modification of Russian society led to the unforeseen birth of an embryonic civil society. People were able to promote intellectual debate in every social class and even displayed overt hostility in their confrontations with the autocracy. A whole generation of intellectuals—men and women, aristocrats and bourgeois—devoted itself to renovating the primary and secondary school systems. Taking advantage of newly acquired freedoms, the universities preventively abolished censure, which in turn led to reforms of the best academic institutions.

The intellectuals and the people energized and radicalized each other. The new Russian elite was extremely diverse, with people like Alexander Herzen, Nikolai Tchernishevsky, Mikhail Bakunin, and Piotr Lavrov, who became the protagonists of the "Slavic Revolution." The vibrant populist movement of the

*T*he Emperor Nikolai II and his family, photographed on August 16, 1901. Upon succeeding Alexander III in 1894, Russia's last Czar, deeply hostile to reform, intended to continue his father's policies. Popular opposition was getting stronger and more confident, though, and only the energetic actions of the Czar's Finance Minister, Sergei Witte, during the first decade of his reign saved the empire from a revolutionary crisis.
Ph © L'Illustration/Sygma

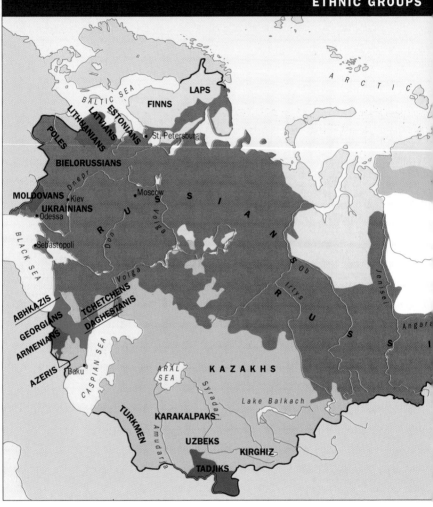

1870s (*narodnishestvo*) produced a multitude of offshoots, some of which organized themselves into political parties. These structures were decidedly Jacobinite in orientation and embraced violence as a justifiable means to achieve social change.

The assassination of Alexander II on March 1, 1881 by the terrorist group Narodnaya Volya caused a violent reaction within the imperial court. The reigns of Alexander III (1881–1894) and Nikolai II (1894–1917) were marked by a flood of counterreforms, draconian

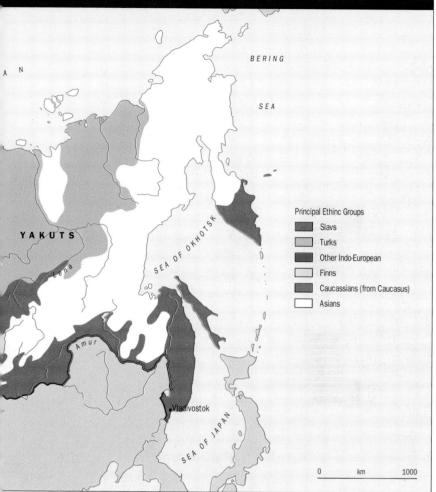

Principal Ethinc Groups

- Slavs
- Turks
- Other Indo-European
- Finns
- Caucassians (from Caucasus)
- Asians

repressive measures, and a significant regression in the level of education for the people, at the same time as the Czars were undertaking an unprecedented, and ill-fated, effort to "Russify" the various ethnic groups of the empire. By the end of the century, Russian absolutism had shown itself to be incapable of facing the challenges of modernization in a society that was already openly embracing them, unwilling to address social unrest that increased unchecked, with its political assassinations and organized agitation, and deaf to the cries of the *zemstvas* demanding more representation. The empire retreated into the manic defense of its own authority, the sole guarantee in its own eyes of stability, order, and military prominence.

The Crisis of the Old Regime

Russian society, in spite of the upheavals subsequent to the emancipation of the serfs, had traversed the greater part of the nineteenth century without seeing the ancient immobility of the feudal system disturbed. It is true that there had been radical change in the political institutions and the social order. It is also true that some progressive aristocrats had favored these reforms and that certain ministers—following the example of Mikail Speranski—had embarked on the path of modernization. But these men had not foreseen the emergence of a social class that was demanding reforms as a cultural and economic necessity, openly labeling the imperial autocracy an impediment to the empire's growth, and criticizing a bureaucracy that was obstinately indifferent to popular sentiment.

The writer Leo Tolstoy (1828–1910) is the late-nineteenth century's great moral authority. Averse to any form of dogmatism, the author of War and Peace *was the ardent defender of all those who were being persecuted for having obeyed the voice of their conscience. Following the success of his novel* Resurrection *he was excommunicated in 1901.
Ph © L'Illustration/Sygma*

From 1880 onward, with Russia launched on a capitalist path of industrial growth, the need for a total renovation of the political system and the dismantlement of the traditional institutions of society was being felt more and more acutely. The nation's participation in the new economic process was still at a low level, with most of the capital remaining in the hands of Western financiers. This slowed the emergence of an internal market. The reality was that Russia's recent evolution necessitated a new form of autonomy for the different sectors of production, and a more open arena for the unstable middle classes, which were becoming increasingly bold in their confrontations with the authorities seeking to limit their freedom of action.

In this context, there appeared an avant-garde, a unified, politically eclectic group of people who shared certain common goals. This united front was comprised of ambitious artisans who wanted to extend their range of operations; merchants who had accumulated wealth and who were waiting for the opportunity to invest this capital in the burgeoning industry; as well as engineers who specialized in key sectors of manufacturing that encouraged technological innovation and scientific progress. There were also some bureaucrats who, thanks to the creation of the *zemstvas*, had attuned themselves to the needs of the social groups taken up in this race to "modern times"; old Christians and

ЦАРЬ, ПОП И БОГАЧ

Jews who had distinguished themselves in the financial or industrial arenas, but who had continued to endure religious persecution; rural capitalists of various provenance, who had made their fortunes after the abolition of serfdom; and finally the industrialists, with their precarious hold on the reins of impatient progress.

This set of actors was still rather small in number and more apolitical than political, but they had found another class of people ready to echo their concerns: the intelligentsia. The intelligentsia was a key element, the true superstructure of Russian society, and it had allied itself to the view that the new economic needs of the bourgeoisie entailed a political response that was the antipode of absolutism—in other words, a regime with a Constitution and a Parliament.

The new alliance between the intelligentsia and the emerging classes—bourgeoisie and workers—was

"The Czar, the Pope, and the Rich Man on the back of the People." This revolutionary poster denounces the "drinkers of blood" of the imperial regime. "Workers and peasants, do you want to give more blood to these predators?... Rise up to defend your power, your lands, and your freedom!"
Ph © BDIC

A workers' strike at the Stroganov factory in Perm (Ural region) at the beginning of the century. Burgeoning capitalism had aggravated the conflicts between manual laborers and factory owners. The proletarian issue was now in the foreground. Initially, workers fought for better wages, but from 1901 and onward the goal—universally embraced by the workers—was an eight-hour workday.
Ph © Novosti

perceived as a distinct threat by the ruling class. The Czarists were to respond by ever more rigid autocratic attitudes, holding to the belief, for example, that industrialization could proceed as a reincarnated form of feudalism, with a multitude of small private cooperatives subservient to large, state-owned factories.

The imperial regime, however, had to face the growing dissatisfaction of the rural population. Peasants were becoming poorer and poorer, in addition to being the victims of new kinds of exploitation. The renowned Russian writer Leo Tolstoy denounced this situation in a letter to the Czar on January 16, 1902 that created a furor, both in Russia and abroad:

"One third of Russia is living under a special regime, one might as well say the law does not apply to them. The power of the police, secret and accounting to no one, grows day by day. The ranks of prisons and penal colonies are bursting, not only with hundreds of thousands of petty criminals, but now with people convicted for offenses of a political nature, many of whom are simple factory workers. Censorship is an added feature of this absurd judicial landscape, the likes of which were unimaginable even in the worst years of the 1840s. Never, as now, has religious persecution been so cruel and so commonplace. In every city, in every industrial center, troops are quartered and regularly unleashed, with live ammunition, against the people. There have been many accounts of fratricidal massacres, and at any rate worse still awaits us just over the horizon. The result of the government's severe repression of the hundred million farmers and peasants upon whom the power of Russia depends is that these people, in spite of an ever-increasing state budget, or perhaps because of this increase, are being dragged down into poverty that just keeps getting worse year after year. Famine has become a banal occurrence, and so has the hostility and general discontent of the people toward the government."

A delegate hears the grievances of a barefoot village representative. After the abolition of serfdom in 1861, the role of the rural community (mir) became crucial as a relay between the state and the peasants, when its administrative functions were officially recognized.
Ph © L'illustration/Sygma

In the spring and summer of 1902, in the wake of failed harvests, there were numerous incidents in the Ukraine and the Volga region pitting peasants against landowners and administrators: fires and destruction of property belonging to the aristocrats, including their houses and granaries, livestock theft, and in some cases, landlords or government functionaries were murdered. The situation was getting out of control, with massive strikes, first among railroad workers, then followed by the factory workers, creating a favorable climate for revolutionary terrorism, an activity that attracted countless students and intellectuals from the petite bourgeoisie.

On February 1, 1901 the Minister of Instruction, Nikolai Bogolepov, was assassinated. On April 2, of the following

In Moscow's Red Square, Muscovites pray for the Russian army, engaged against the Japanese in Manchuria. The surrender of Port Arthur on December 20, 1904 was a direct cause of the great revolt of 1905.

Ph © L'Illustration/Sygma

year, the same fate befell the Minister of the Interior, Dimitri Sipyagin. The clearest signal of the disturbance level attained by the armed wing of the socialist revolutionary movement came on July 15, 1904, with the killing of Vyacheslav Pleve, a powerful governmental figure, on the street in broad daylight. Other events compounded the turmoil: in 1904, as a result of its expansionist policies in the East, Russia went to war. Russia had been countering Japan's efforts to increase

THE RUSSO-JAPANESE

One of the first modern conflicts, the Russo-Japanese War had a devastating psychological effect on Russian soldiers. Leonid Andreyev's short story, "The Red Laugh," offers precious firsthand testimony:

"The battle is in its eighth day now. It started last Friday. Saturday passed, then Sunday, Monday, Tuesday, Wednesday, Thursday. Friday came and went. But the battle rages on. The two armies,

totaling several hundred thousand men, tear at each other without quarter, canons go off without the slightest interruption. Each minute, human beings brimming with life become corpses. The constant vibration makes the sky shake, and black, filthy clouds drift above the soldiers' heads. But they fight on, never retreating, always killing. When a man goes for 72 hours without sleep, he falls unconscious, loses his memory.

These men have been awake for a week, and they have gone mad. They will not surrender, will not retreat, but will fight on until the last man is dead. There have been stories of units that have run out of ammunition, and take up stones to throw at the enemy...

"If these men in tatters were to return home, they would have fangs like wolves. But they will not return. They have all been killed, and they

its influence in the Korean peninsula, and penetrating further into Manchuria thanks to the new Trans-Siberian Railroad. This, as well as the installation of a naval base at Port Arthur, contributed to the strained relations between the two countries. Encouraged by business owners intent on expanding their own activity in the Orient, the war was also seen by the Czarists as an expedient means to quell revolutionary agitation once and for all.

In fact, the conflict failed utterly to produce a spark of

WAR (1904-1905)

have killed all. Or, murdered souls walk on still-living legs. Everything is topsy-turvy for them, they can no longer understand the simplest things. If someone bumps into them, they will wheel about and turn their guns on their comrades, shooting at the enemy in their mind's eye. They hear strange voices, speak only in whispers, their pallid faces the exact image of primal terror and dread. Brother, oh brother, listen to what they're saying about the red laughter! It is as if there had appeared on the battle-field full legions of ghosts, regi-ments of phantoms, usurpers of hearts that still beat. At night, when the exhausted men collapse for a few moments of sleep, or during the day in the heat of battle, when the clear sky has been darkened by the guns, these shadows spring up suddenly, along with weapons of their own. Then the men, crazed by the real and imaginary cannons' roar, fight their doubled enemies until the last drop of blood is on the ground... The phantoms retreat, and there is a momen-tary calm around the place where a man lived. The ground is covered with mutilated bodies. Who killed them? Do you know, brother, who killed them?"

L. Andreyev, "The Red Laugh," Znanie, St. Petersburg 1905.

national unity. Public opinion saw hostility against Japan as an ill-disguised, derivative form of colonialism of little importance, which could in no way serve to justify the empire's domestic policies. As for the foot soldiers marching toward Manchuria, they felt very little personal interest in the outcome of the fight.

The war in the East was waged imprudently and with insufficient preparation, and it resulted in an enormous waste of human lives and resources. The bloody defeats at Port Arthur, Mukden, and Tsushima completely discredited the ambitions of the Czar, opening the path to

St. Petersburg, January 9, 1905: The army fires upon civilians carrying a petition demanding reforms to the Czar. "Bloody Sunday" marks the beginning of the movement Lenin referred to as having enacted a "general rehearsal" for the events of 1917. The proletariat or industrialized working class in the background of the photograph is going through its baptism of fire in one of its first general strikes. Ph © L'Illustration/Sygma

revolution for the Russian people and Russian society.

The Revolution of 1905

At the end of 1904, the friction between the new civil society and representatives of the ancient feudal order came to a head. The *ukaz* (decree) promulgated by Nikolai II on December 12 sought to allay the tension with a few modest concessions toward groups representing the emerging classes. But in spite of political and fiscal measures, and gestures toward workers' unions and the clergy, the decree did not even broach the issue of a national assembly, nor did it imply that the Czar was considering the idea of a constitution. In only a few days, events would crystallize that revealed the strength of the new opposition movement. Indeed, the sphere of influence of the opposition had considerably enlarged.

The principal result of the changes wrought by the introduction of capitalism in Russia was that industrial workers in the big cities joined unions in massive numbers and soon became politicized. On January 3, 1905, following a layoff, workers at the Putilov factory

THE SPREAD OF MARXISM IN RUSSIA

Karl Marx wrote these lines to his friend, Ludwig Kugelman on October 12, 1868:

"A few days ago, I received the surprising news from a publisher in St. Petersburg that the Russian translation of *Capital* was going to press. He asked for a photograph of me for the title page, and I couldn't deny 'my dear Russian friends' this small service.

"It is certainly an irony of fate that the Russians—whom I have fought against for twenty-five years, in German, in English, and in French—remain ever my truest supporters. In the years 1843–44, in Paris, I was the mascot of the Russian aristocracy there."

Marx emphasized the warm reception that his first writings had enjoyed in Russia. "Russia is therefore to be the first foreign country to translate *Capital*. One must not overestimate the importance of this fact. Young aristocrats today finish their education in German or Parisian universities, and they feel strongly drawn to everything extreme the West produces." Indeed, the first translation of *Capital* came out in 1872, less than five years after its publication in Germany—and fifteen years before the first English translation.

Marx's ideas began to spread in Russia through the populists, in fact a loose gathering of groups that had become involved in theories promoting a rural revolution, and that condoned terrorism against representatives of the Czar. The populists were profoundly impressed by Marx's account of the atrocities that were a result of the rapid growth of capital and the Industrial Revolution in Britain. They adhered completely to his analysis of economic surplus and his critique of the political economy. However, they hesitated before the evolutionary thesis of capitalism, according to which this new economic order represented not only the next stage in the progress of autocracy, but also in that of society as a whole. Yuri Plekhanov (1856–1918) was the first man to break with the populists on this point, by recognizing the truth behind the idea that capitalism was a context that had facilitated the growth of the revolutionary movement. In 1883, together with Pavel Axelrod and Vera Zasulich, he founded the first Russian Marxist organization, in Switzerland: it was called "Workers' Emancipation." This revolutionary group's program laid the foundations of social democracy for Russia, and envisioned the creation of a workers' party within the Czar's empire. In the years following, numerous Marxist reviews sprouted up. In 1895 in St. Petersburg, the first issue of "Unified in the struggle for the liberation of the working class" came out. Among the signatures was that of a certain Vladimir Illych Ulianov, later to become known as Lenin. ∎

The despair of a Jewish man of Lodz after the violence of June 1905. From 1903 to 1906, anti-Semitic pogroms fomented by right-wing extremist factions were regular occurrences, and claimed hundreds of victims. The Czar overtly encouraged this violent persecution, calling them "demonstrations of patriotism."
Ph © L'Illustration/Sygma

in St. Petersburg went on strike. The work stoppage quickly spread to other factories and took on the allure of a general strike, with the participation of about 250,000 workers. The organization behind the strike was the Union of Factory Workers, created by the state, and the man at the head of this union was a young priest, Yuri Gapon. The petition he addressed to the Czar bore over 135,000 signatures.

It was in fact a very polite request for economic and political reforms, couched in the traditional phrasing of popular grievances humbly brought to the attention of the Imperial Czar:

"We, the workers of the city of St. Petersburg, with our wives, our children, and our poor old parents, have come to you, our Lord, in quest of justice and protection. We have been reduced to misery; we live oppressed, broken by labor beyond our human strength. We are looked upon with contempt, as if we were not human beings. We are being treated like slaves, who should suffer their bitter fate in silence. And we have borne all this bravely, but we are being thrust ever further downward, to unspeakable depths of poverty and ignorance. Despotism and arbitrariness kill by suffocation, and we are dying of suffocation. Our strength is almost at an end, Lord, and our patience exhausted. We are united in this terrible moment, in which death is preferable to a life of unrelenting pain."

On January 9, 1905, the people of St. Petersburg were called to demonstrate in front of the Winter Palace. Over 140,000 men, women, and children filled the streets of the ancient city. Carrying religious icons and chanting hymns, they planned to take their petition to the Czar. But the imperial troops fired upon the crowd, killing several hundred and wounding over two thousand civilians. And "Bloody Sunday," as it came to be known, destroyed the last trust the people still had in the Czar's benevolence.

The Revolution of 1905 thus began. The Minister of the Interior, underestimating the state of tension

between the people and the authorities, had declared that any unauthorized demonstration was to be forcibly repressed. But the brutality the authorities displayed led to uprisings all over the empire.

Solidarity strikes spontaneously occurred in most of the big industrial centers of the country. The main political groupings, already used to clandestine communication and rapid mobilization of forces, went into action. The revolutionary socialists who came onto the scene in 1901–2 had inherited the specifically Russian tradition of "populism," and counted heavily on the movement's extension into the countryside. But the Russian Social Democrats were fraught with division. From the formation of their party in Minsk in 1898, unity lasted until the Double Congress of Brussels–London in 1903. By then, two factions had emerged: the majority Bolshevik group, with a revolutionary program and professional politicians leading the fight, and the minority Mensheviks, who tended toward more evolutionary thinking and were more attentive to the material needs of the workers at the base of the movement.

On April 27, 1905, Nikolai II solemnly opens the first parliament in Russia's history, the Duma, in St. George's Room at the Winter Palace in St. Petersburg. But the Assembly had little chance to exercise its prerogatives, since it was dissolved in the summer of the same year. The opposition parties responded by calling on the people to refuse military service and to stop paying their taxes.
Ph © L'Illustration/Sygma

With the 1905 uprising crushed, it's back to politics as usual: here, the landed gentry are gathered to select candidates for the elections to the Duma scheduled for February 20, 1907. The far left was to see its ranks reinforced, with 65 social-democratic representatives in the so-called "Red Duma."
Ph © L'Illustration/Sygma

Other parties were created as a consequence of the revolution. The Octobrists (Members of the Union of October 17) in 1905, and the Popular Socialists and the Trudoviki (Workers' Group) in 1906. The Cadets, constitutional democrats, also formalized their political existence in 1905, thanks to the fusion of the Union for Liberation and the Union of Constitutional *zemstvas*. This became the most important party of the center, with a fairly modern program that could entice away from the opposition certain sectors of progressive aristocrats who were intensely aware of the extent of the dissolution affecting their own class.

Beside the new parties, autonomous unions appeared. The printers' union was the first to enter the political arena. Their recruitment base gave them a ready supply of men from the myriad "workers' defense" groups that had sprung up spontaneously in the factories. In the meantime, the student population—having obtained the Decree of August 26 granting autonomy to the universities—had turned academic institutions into powerful organizational nuclei within the vast movement of opposition; the revolution was to go forth bedecked with committees and commissions. The most successful structures of militancy were the soviets,

elected governmental councils, which had acquired a certain experience in democratic practices. Their innovation was to copy the age-old system of peasant assemblies, the *mir*: this reference was immediately tangible to the factory workers, for the most part still culturally ensconced in rural patterns of life. The first soviet in Russian history was created in May 1905 at the Ivanovo–Voznesenk factory, a major manufacturer of textiles of the Moscow area. It was followed a few weeks later by the Kostromo Workers' Soviet.

From the cities, the revolt spread spontaneously to the countryside, with a rallying cry that gained in volume each day: the socialization of the land—in other words, that the land should be distributed to the tenant farmers who cultivated it with their own hands. From February onward, peasants from various provinces (Orel, Kursk, Chernigov), began to seize the property of landowners, not hesitating to use force. These actions on the part of the revolutionary socialists demonstrated the commitment of the rural base, and gave a decisive impetus to a movement that had started out as a scattering of loosely organized, but highly intense political energies.

At the height of the uprising, Russian cities and rural areas were at the boiling point. In October, railroad workers in Moscow launched a huge strike: in place of the traditional, wage-oriented demands common to both factory workers and tenant farmers, explicitly political ones now rang out stridently. In spite of many attempts at establishing a dialogue, urban and rural movements never managed to cooperate, although a certain rapport was initiated with the soldiers and sailors in the period between the end of hostilities with Japan and June 1905. Disappointed members of the military grimly adhered to the new demands being voiced all over Russia, and many joined the ranks of the socialists.

Finally, the revolution radiated outward, involving the

Piotr Stolypin, Prime Minister after the dissolution of the first Duma, dissolved the second Duma in June 1907, in an unambiguous display of autocratic guilt. As artisan of the Czarist reaction, he devised and implemented important agrarian reforms that enabled a new class of landed peasants to emerge. He was assassinated in September 1911 by a double agent, a member of the Czar's secret police (Okrana) who was also a revolutionary socialist. Ph © L'Illustration/Sygma

The repression was unrelenting under Stolypin's rule when hundreds of revolutionaries were condemned to death by special tribunals. Here, a group of convicts departs for Siberia. A woman proudly sticks out her tongue at the photographer.
Ph © L'Illustration/Sygma

farthest reaches of the empire. The non-Russian provinces were the theater of the most violent events of the 1905 revolution: Poland, Georgia, Finland, and the Baltic region. The Ukrainian revolutionary movement breathed new life, and elsewhere Lithuanians, Belarusians, and Muslims were organizing themselves in new ways and meeting in assemblies. Old ambitions of political autonomy re-emerged to combine with the new goal of social emancipation in a beleaguered empire that was multiethnic, multinational, and multilingual. The Czar's strategy, however, was to continue to instigate violence on the periphery of the empire, in particular pogroms against the Jews, but also against Armenians in the Ukraine and in Romania—ostensibly to redirect the people's anger.

The various socialist groups participated in the revolution with different, and often opposed, interests. But they all seemed to share at least one common vision: that of a national assembly. This idea was repeated endlessly in propaganda diffused by a press that managed to almost completely avoid censorship. Soon the Czar could no longer deny that the revolution was a reality, a phenomenon that involved every social class and every ethnic group in the empire. The new Minister of the Interior, Bulygin, proposed establishing a duma, a legislative assembly with representatives from the various classes; the Czar ratified it on August 6, 1905.

This attempt at reforming the political institutions met with a poor welcome among the opposition, for the Duma had no real legislative power; moreover, many ethnic groups were not given a vote in the Assembly. Three months later, through the pen of his

Prime Minister, Wittel, the Czar established a list of fundamental civil rights: inviolability of the individual, and freedom of the press, of speech, to assemble, and to form parties. He also granted the vote to all nationalities within the empire, and gave the Duma the power to approve the laws of the State.

Most Russians enthusiastically received this October Manifesto, as the reforms were called. But it would have been a mistake to believe that the end of absolutism was near. At no time did the Czar ever mention the possibility of a constitution or a constitutional regime. The main consequence of the manifesto was to polarize further an opposition already bitterly divided. On the one hand, the moderates, who were content with what had already been obtained, saw in the political reforms a new impetus for the cause of economic liberalism. On the contrary, the radicals' plan was to push for social reforms right away, and its proponents had no intention of laying down arms until absolutism was totally vanquished. As for the reactionary forces, they were on high alert following the October Manifesto's diffusion. The "Black Centurions" (Chernosotentsy), openly supported by the secret police (Okrana), resumed their persecution of

In the years following the 1905 revolution, the empire was shaken by chronic political violence. A bomb killed Colonel Karpov, Chief of Police of St. Petersburg, in December 1910. Here, the owner of the establishment Karpov, who was tricked into visiting, assesses the damage from the explosion on the floor above.
Ph © L'Illustration/Sygma

intellectuals and workers, as well as the pogroms against Jews. In the week following October 18, violent incidents in nearly all urban centers resulted in at least 3,500 dead, and over 10,000 wounded.

The radical opposition disposed of a multitude of strike committees in each of the principal cities of the empire and reorganized them as soviets. These began to fulfill an administrative role for the public and spearheaded an untiring political struggle. The soviet of St. Petersburg, established on October 13, was the most prominent among them: it succeeded in becoming a veritable parliament for the working class. By the end of October, the conflict had reached a fever pitch. Soldiers and sailors mutinied, the countryside was in turmoil, and railroad strikes paralyzed the empire from one end to the other.

The peasants, least organized of the forces in play, gave in first, allowing the government to regain control of the situation. In a mere two months, the Czarist troops were redeployed to the cities, where revolutionaries had put together an armed resistance. From then on, the empire quickly recovered lost terrain and the Czar was finally able to quell completely the opposition movement with a series of brutal punitive measures.

Following the revolutionaries' defeat, the Czar was determined to restore absolutism to its pre-1905 glory. He took back the powers delegated to the National Assembly and abrogated the reforms of October 17. Furthermore, the State Council was henceforth the organ by which the Czar gave himself the right to veto the laws approved by the Chamber of Deputies, and to promulgate acts independently of the National Assembly. However, this could hardly be said to constitute a return to the status quo of absolutism before the events of 1905. The idea of a constitution (the "Fundamental Law") had been aired at last, and the Duma's official existence was reestablished in April 1906.

Russia finally had its first parliament. Its almost immediate dissolution, on July 9, 1906 only proved the inexorable vitality of the more radical sectors of the opposition. The Second Duma (February 20–June 3, 1907)—also known as the "Red Duma" because of the participation of certain Bolsheviks—would meet the same fate. The Third Duma, whose representatives were elected according to a new set of rules, embodied the government's ambition to reestablish once more an autocratic political system: the landed gentry of the right regained privileges and predominance, through this "Duma of the Lords" (November 1, 1907–June 9, 1912). From November 15, 1912, the Fourth Duma gave itself the task of rolling the government's initiatives onto the bureaucracy. The First World War was just around the corner when the imperial court decided to disallow all debate on constitutional matters.

The turn of the century had produced a tumultuous decade, in which Russia gained the experience of a semblance of democracy, with parliaments of one sort or another in the fore of the political scene, and an opposition that was not about to give up its struggle against autocracy.

Between 1897 and 1905, Lenin, prototype of the professional revolutionary, was jailed, deported to Siberia, and then exiled. After a brief return to St. Petersburg in 1905 during the revolution, he went abroad again two years later, where he stayed until April of 1917.
Ph © L'Illustration/Sygma

OCCUPATION: REVOLUTIONARY

Vladimir Illych Ulyanov, a.k.a. Lenin (1870–1924), was born in Simbirsk to a school inspector father whose sons were all revolutionaries. In 1887, Vladimir was just entering the University of Kazan to study law, only to be expelled following a student revolt. In 1891, he obtained his diploma in jurisprudence from St. Petersburg University as an external candidate. Settling in the capital, he fought against populism and helped distribute Marxist propaganda in the factory workers' milieu. In 1895, he met Plekhanov in Switzerland and, once back in Russia, participated in the founding of the "Union for the struggle for workers' emancipation." Arrested, he spent a year in jail, and then was sentenced to deportation to Siberia for three years.

In 1900, free, he left Russia with the intention of contributing to the development of the social-democratic party by publishing a newsletter to be clandestinely distributed in Russia. Plekhanov agreed to collaborate in this venture; in December 1900, the first issue of *Iskra* (The Spark) came out in Stuttgart, followed soon after by a review devoted to Marxist theory, *Zarja* (The Dawn). In 1902, Lenin published *What Is to Be Done?* in which he propounded the creation of a centralized organization of professional revolutionaries, few in number, whose function would be to represent the avant-garde of the working class.

In this extract, Lenin spells out the roles and attributes of this revolutionary elite: "I assert: 1) that no revolutionary movement can endure without a stable organization of leaders maintaining continuity; 2) that the broader the popular mass drawn spontaneously into the struggle, which forms the basis of the movement and participates in it, the more urgent the need for such an organization... 3) that such an organization must consist chiefly of people professionally engaged in revolutionary activity; 4) that in an autocratic state, the more we confine the membership of such an organization to people...who have been professionally trained in the art of combating the political police, the more difficult it will be to unearth the organization..." The success of the October Revolution put Lenin at the head of the Sovnarkom (Soviet of the Commissariat of the People). From this point Lenin's biography coincides with that of the government of Soviet Russia.

V.I. Lenin, *What Is to Be Done?*
∎

Chapter 2

THE 1917 REVOLUTION

DRAGGED INTO THE WAR, RUSSIA FALLS INTO CHAOS. IN 1917, DURING THE "DAYS OF FEBRUARY," THE CZAR IS DEPOSED; IN OCTOBER, THE BOLSHEVIKS TRIUMPHANTLY TAKE POWER.

When war broke out in 1914, Russia was tightly bound to France by a naval alliance that had solidified pacts and trade agreements made in the 1890s. Representatives of Russian railroads had just returned from Paris where tenders had been posted for the development of the national railway. Russia had also considerably improved relations with England, thanks to the Russo–British Pact of August 18, 1907 pertaining to zones of influence in Asia (Iran, Afghanistan, Tibet) and staking out mutually recognized interests of the two countries in the region. On the other hand, recent events in the Balkans had aggravated tension between Russia and Austria-Hungary, and German interference in Turkish affairs led to new bones of contention with Russia.

In this context, Russia saw fit to deploy concerted efforts to strengthen its ties with France and England. There was, to be sure, a faction sympathetic to Germany within the Russian aristocracy that considered the German monarchy a model of government more closely aligned to their absolutist penchants. But the Czar suppressed these leanings relentlessly and staunchly reasserted Russia's friendship with the Allied powers by declaring war on Germany on July 18, 1914.

With Russia stepping in on the side of the Western democracies, the governments of Central Europe had to fight a war on two fronts, transferring huge forces to the East. However, while the Western powers could rely on a heavily industrialized economic apparatus, which they

"Glory to women in the struggle for freedom!" The revolution began with the commemoration of International Women's Day on February 23 (March 8 according to our calendar). The demonstrators had no definite plan at this stage, and no political party was ready for a big fight. But in 1917, the imperial regime was at such a level of decadence and weakness that it could no longer control the people, nor could it quell their protests against despotism and the war.
Ph © L'Illustration/Sygma

had prepared for the war effort well before hostilities broke out, Russia's military was totally unprepared for a conflict of such magnitude. From August 13 to August 17 of 1914, the Russian army, led by two generals, Rennenkampf and Samsonov, faced a massive German assault at Tannenberg. The defeat of the Russians was so crushing that over 100,000 men were captured. This was only the first of a series of spectacular routs. From May to October 1915, over 150,000 Russians were killed, and over a million were wounded or taken prisoner. In two years, an army that had mobilized millions of men—although without being able to supply them with the most essential equipment beyond a weapon—was in a state of near total collapse.

By the end of 1916, Russia was in the grip of runaway inflation. With the casualties of war and the unraveling of the social fabric, it had become ungovernable. Relations between urban and rural populations, always precarious, became overtly hostile. The rural masses and the urban proletariat displayed deep, mutual resentment. Nevertheless, they were momentarily united in their opposition to the war. Protests and strikes were chronic, and met with brutal repression and the abolition of political and union-related freedoms. The signs of a crisis of authority were all too apparent. Troops were mutinying and refusing to fire on demonstrators, and the police was losing men. Everywhere there was talk of revolt, insurrection, and revolution.

The Days of February

A multitude of factors played a part in the February Revolution: the domino-style chaos caused by organized strikes and spontaneous popular uprisings, soldiers turning their weapons on their officers, and politicians vituperating against a government incapable of governing the country. There was less and less food, and the hungry Russian population was already influenced by anti-war propaganda. In mid-February of 1917, the public granary of Petrograd (called St. Petersburg until 1914) had a ten-day supply of flour left. When the military authorities announced the introduction of rationing coupons, people lined up for hours in front of the shops, or found them empty when their turn finally came up. There were

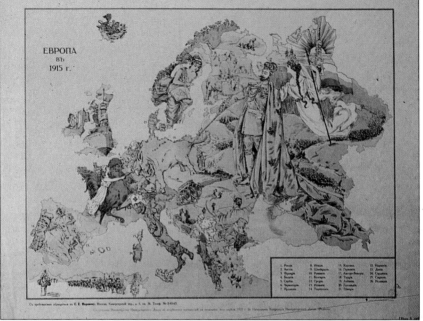

СИМВОЛИЧЕСКАЯ КАРТА ЕВРОПЫ

ЕВРОПА
въ
1915 г.

incidents in different parts of the city. On February 22, workers protesting massive layoffs paralyzed the Putilov factory complex with a lockout, forcing the Czar to rush back from his headquarters.

The Days of February (February 23–27) signaled the final crisis of the Czarist regime. Remarkable for the unexpected rapidity with which the workers mobilized, the uprising began on February 23, International Women's Day (March 8 by our calendar). Roughly 90,000 striking workers joined the parade of women; the next day, the strikers' ranks had swelled to roughly 200,000 people, with many more in the streets. By the 25th, nearly all workers were on strike.

The authorities grossly underestimated the magnitude of the workers' demands for new reforms: they were not to be satisfied with distributions of bread and flour alone. The first clashes between soldiers and demonstrators were bloody. On February 26, gunfire sounded throughout the city. There were over 150 deaths, but soldiers had begun to fraternize with the workers, and to desert their units. The government

Allegorical map of Europe in 1915. The outbreak of war initially provoked a "Sacred Union"; every party with the notable exception of the Bolsheviks threw itself into the fight against the hereditary enemy, Germany. But in the space of months, military defeat and penury imposed on the population created a chaos that completely overshadowed the international conflict.
Ph © BDIC

decreed a state of siege in Petrograd.

Mikhail Rodzianko vainly begged the Czar to make concessions and to allow the formation of a new government, headed by someone capable of winning back the people's trust. February 27 was the decisive day of the Revolution. Following mutinies in several regiments (Pavlovski, Preobrajenski, Litovski, Volynski, Semenovski), soldiers and workers occupied the Fortress of Peter and Paul and freed all the political prisoners. They also pillaged the arsenal, making off with guns and ammunition. In a few hours, Petrograd had fallen to the insurgents.

When, on the eve of the Revolution, Nicholas Golytsin had announced to the Duma the Czar's intention to dissolve it, there was a general outcry against the decree, which led to the creation of a "committee for the restoration of order and for the betterment of relations in government." The Duma was also to host the first soviet of workers and soldiers, mostly made up of

socialist revolutionaries, Mensheviks, and people with no party affiliation. On March 2, the committees of the Duma and the new soviet agreed to work together to create a temporary government with a liberal majority, pending the convocation of a constituent assembly.

George Lvov, leader of the Federation of Cities and of the Union of Zemstvas, was chosen to head the new government, and named Minister of the Interior. In the cabinet were the "cadets": Paul Miliukov (Foreign Affairs), Nikolai Nekrassov (Minister of Transportation), Alexander Manuilov (Education), Andrei Chingarev (Agriculture), and Fyodor Rodichev (Finland Affairs); the "Octobrists" Alexander Guchov (Army and Navy), Ivan Godnev (State Comptroller); and other personalities such as Alexander Konovalov (Industry and Trade), a member of the progressive bloc, M.I. Tereschenko (Finance), an independent, Alexander Kerenski (Justice), a former labor party member soon to join the socialist revolutionary camp, and finally Vladimir Lvov (High Officer

The workers of the Putilov steel mill in Petrograd, who had been active in the 1905 Revolution, were to spearhead the February revolution of 1917. During the First World War, there had been 42 strikes at the Putilov foundry, with roughly 160,000 workers participating.
Ph © L'Illustration/Sygma

On February 28, 1917, Petrograd fell to the insurgents, following mutinies in the army and fraternization of soldiers and workers. The Czar's abdication, on March 5, put a definitive end to the Russian monarchy.
Ph © L'Illustration/Sygma

of the Holy Sinod), a conservative.

On March 7, the new government delivered a warrant for the Czar's arrest, in the following terms:

"1. The abdicating Emperor and his wife are to be deprived of liberty and brought to Czarskoie Selo.

2. General Alexeyev is to be given the mission to supply men to the delegates of the Duma (Bibikov, Verchinin, Gribunin, Kalinin) and dispatched to Moghilev to ensure the ex-Czar's surveillance.

3. The delegates of the Duma sent to Moghilev, who are to accompany the ex-Czar to Czarskoie Selo, will make a full report on the fulfilment of their mission to the Duma upon their return.

4.This report is to be made public."

The abdication of Nikolai II, and the Grand Duke Mikhail's refusal to succeed him, left Russia without a sovereign leader. The nation was, however, spared a new epoch of chaos, in spite of the harsh and dangerous political and social climate. This was due to an historic alliance—one of the most important myths in the history of the twentieth century—between the soldiers and the workers of Petrograd. The elected soviet made up of representatives of these two groups constituted a nexus of power that succeeded in preventing the temporary government from becoming a surrogate of the imperial cabinet, which aimed to restore order and continue the war effort until victory was achieved. The workers and soldiers managed to establish a continuity between the January 1905 revolution and that of February 1917. All of the soviets created after February, in the cities as well as in the countryside, were based on the model of the Petrograd Soviet, and had the same functions: control of the army and navy, the roads and railways, and the mail and telegraph.

This was the embodiment of the "duality of power" (*dvoevlastie*): on one side, the temporary government, legitimate expression of the people's will in the last Duma; on the other, the Soviets, who claimed a more direct, local, and therefore truer representation. As soon as a discrepancy appeared in the stated positions or interest of these two powers, permanent conflict would ensue. But for the moment, any differences remained beneath the surface, as the temporary government echoed the

Delegate of the Fourth Duma under Alexander Stolypin's government, Alexander Kerenski was a highly popular proponent of democratic ideas. After the Revolution, he played a key role in the liquidation of the last remnants of Czarism.
Ph © L'Illustration/Sygma

FEBRUARY'S MAN

Alexander Fyodorovich Kerenski (1881–1970) became one of the major figures in the February revolution, through his role in the inception and subsequent consolidation of the "duality of power." He entered politics as a lawyer, and defended several of the 1905 revolutionaries arrested by the Czar's police. Delegate of the Fourth Duma (1912) and close to the revisionist socialist revolutionaries, he joined the Trudoviki (Labor) faction. On February 27, he was elected Vice-President of the Soviet of Petrograd; on March 2, he became Minister of Justice, a

position from which he fought to defend the temporary government. A brilliant orator, his popularity with workers and soldiers diminished when he came out in favor of the war against Germany. However, he was nominated Minister of War (May–July) and, on July 24, Prime Minister, although the political situation was now gravely compromised by military defeat and the Bolsheviks' surging influence. He requested and was granted extraordinary power to reestablish order, but was unable to save the democratic revolution from its fate. Overthrown during the events

of October, he left Petrograd, and, after a failed attempt to recover control of the city, left Russia in 1918. Abroad, Kerenski remained intensely active in political movements opposed to the Soviet regime, but was also the target of ultraconservative Russian émigrés, who held him responsible for the Czarist army's defeat. He is the author of *The Russian Revolution* (Paris, 1928) ∎

Before the revolution: In the Chamber of the Duma, above the President's chair, a portrait of Nikolai II by Ilya Repin dominates the discussions.
Ph © L'Illustration/Sygma

policies of the Petrograd Soviet.

In the context of the First World War, the February Revolution threatened to have potentially catastrophic repercussions on the German and Austro-Hungarian Empires. The contagion of political freedom wrested from the absolutist monarchy in Russia could give a new impetus to the Allies in the war. Aware of this possibility, the German government allowed an armored train filled with mostly Bolshevik revolutionaries—and Lenin—to cross the country on its way to Russia. The Germans were well informed as to the stance of the Russian social democrats regarding the continuation of war, and had been following their progress very attentively since the beginning of the Revolution. They relied on the destabilizing effects of pacifist Bolshevik propaganda on a people already hostile to the war effort.

On April 4, Lenin presented his famous "April Theses" to the Bolsheviks gathered in a legal assembly. The ten points of this manifesto elucidated the communist platform that would be adopted, with a few adjustments, after the October Revolution: suppression of the police, the army, and the entire corps of state functionaries, confiscation of the landed gentry's property—all land would belong to the State—and creation of a national bank; control of production and distribution of goods would also fall to the soviets. In truth, the April Theses sought to solve the problem of power shared by the soviets and the government. In Lenin's view, a transition period characterized by a parliamentary regime supported by the proletariat, was futile. Proponent of total opposition to the temporary government, Lenin stigmatized the democratic, bourgeois phase of the revolution and demanded total power for the soviets. But the government saw in Lenin's expressed wish to disrupt the institutional equilibrium the hand of foreign powers, and accused him of being a German agent.

After the failure of a violent insurrection in July, the Bolsheviks were outlawed. Several leaders were arrested, and Lenin was forced to flee to Finland. But when, at the end of August, General Lavr Kornilov attempted a coup and set his troops on Petrograd, it was the mobilization of the Bolsheviks that saved the day. The party's prestige grew considerably thanks to this exploit: soon, Bolshevik militants succeeded in obtaining majorities in the soviets of Russia's major cities. On September 9, 1917, Leo Trotsky, just out of prison, was elected President of the Soviet of Petrograd.

After: On the second day of the Revolution, the portrait of the Czar was taken down and the chamber occupied by soldiers. The ease with which the Czar was overthrown was a testament to the extreme weakness of a regime in its death throes.
Ph © L'Illustration/Sygma

The Bolsheviks Take Power

Petrograd, October 1917: the Bolsheviks are rumored to be planning an insurrection. The writer Maxim Gorky, editor of *Novaya Szizn* (New Life), an influential but independent socialist review, posts a warning to the people in an unusually violent editorial: "The basest instincts of a people in its folly, aggravated by the

Nikolai II, imprisoned at Tsarskoie Selo. Amid rumors of the imperial family's imminent flight to England, the executive committee of the Petrograd Soviet decided to arrest the Czar. On March 9, 1917, the temporary government ratified and made public a warrant for his arrest.
Ph © L'Illustration/Sygma

disintegration of daily life, the falsehoods and the mudslinging in politics, will ignite and explode, and their awakened ire will stink of resentment and vengeance. Men, incapable as they are of conquering their bestial stupidity, will start killing each other. A random crowd, not knowing what it wants to do, will take to the streets. And adventurers, thieves and professional assassins will use this idiotic fury to go about their mission of "making the history of the Russian Revolution."

Gorki's voice was not the only one. Much of the democratic intelligentsia was hostile to the idea of an insurrection, fearing the consequences of letting the radicals take power on the country's future evolution after such a long period of subjection under serfdom. The legitimacy of a socialist revolution and its feasibility was at the center of intense debate. People were wondering about the economic—and political—maturity of Russian capitalism, as well as the maturity of the former subjects of the Czar who were to be the protagonists of this revolution. According to Gorki, for example, the people's moral culture had first to be brought up to date in order for the intelligentsia in its entirety to link up their fates with theirs. This would take time. Otherwise, political and social upheaval would not lead to durable and positive change; thus, the revolution was to be avoided at all costs.

In the eyes of the Bolsheviks, the success of the revolution was not dependent on cultural issues; on the contrary, the revolution itself—shattering historical continuity—would create the material conditions necessary to pulverize backwardness and change people's mentalities. Educating the people day by day and slowly weaning them away from the traditional ways of life and archaic knowledge of an agrarian and pagan world would not suffice to bring them out of the darkness of superstition and into the light of reason. Only the revolution could transform the Russian peasant, facilitate the spread of an industrial mentality, and bring about the triumph of modernity.

Moral literacy had not been a factor in the spread of a social democratic awareness; the modernization of the entire structure of production in Russia was, however, because it had already inculcated the new mentality in all those it affected, giving them the wherewithal to live in a new society. In other words, people could not be changed through incremental evolution of mentalities and the slow disintegration of the old ways: only the

"THE SCYTHIANS"

Most Russian intellectuals manifested open hostility toward the Revolution, with the notable exception of writers with ties to the literary and philosophical current known as "Scythism" (*skifstvo*). In this view, the Revolution was a universal cataclysm, precondition to a rebirth of the spirit, a purifying fire that would annihilate a doomed social order. In his diary, Alexander Blok, the poet, wrote: "For several days, I could physically hear an incredible din wherever I turned, perhaps the sound of the ancient order of things collapsing."

His poem, "The Twelve," achieved considerable notoriety: it depicted twelve Red Guards plodding through the snow at night, with guns drawn, preceded unbeknownst to them by an invisible Christ wearing a crown of roses. At the end of January 1918, Blok composed "The Scythians" in two days, published two months

later in the socialist revolutionary review, *Znamja Truda* (Workers' Standard). In it, he extols the "barbarism" of the East, as opposed to the decadence of the West.

"Pan-Mongolism – though the word is strange,
My ear acclaims its gongs."
—Vladimir Solovyov

You are the millions, we are the multitude
And multitude and multitude.
Come, fight! Yea, we are Scythians,
Yea, Asians, a squint-eyed, greedy brood.

For you: the centuries; for us: one hour.
Like slaves, obeying and abhorred,
We were the shield between the breeds
Of Europe and the raging Mongol horde...

For centuries your eyes were turned to the East.
Our pearls you horded in your chests,

And mockingly you bode the day
When you could aim your cannon at our breasts.

The time has come! Disaster beats its wings.
With every day the insults grow.
The hour will strike, and without ruth
Your proud and powerless Paestums will be laid low.

Oh pause, old world, while life still beats in you.
Oh weary one, oh worn, oh wise!
Halt here, as once did Oedipus

Before the Sphinx's enigmatic eyes.
Yea, Russia is a Sphinx.
Exulting, grieving,
And sweating blood, she cannot sate
Her eyes that gaze and gaze
At you with stone-lipped love for you, and hate. ∎

Anti-war demonstration, Petrograd, May 1917. In spite of the temporary government's efforts to remobilize the army at the front, the catastrophic paralysis of supplies, the growing agitation of the workers, and the absence of agrarian reform reinforced the Soviets' authority and the Bolsheviks' pacifist propaganda.
Ph © L'Illustration/Sygma

revolution would accomplish this.

Discussions of insurrection had become so widely publicized that a decision had to be made. Lenin maintained pressure for the Bolsheviks to move into action without hesitation and call for an armed uprising. The recent events of July and the coup attempt of August were clear evidence for the Bolshevik leader that the future of the Revolution was not in the hands of the soviets. The workers had to take up the reins of the country's destiny. Power had to be seized: it was time for the dictatorship of the proletariat.

The Bolsheviks put into action an intense campaign of political agitation, which produced excellent results. The task was relatively easy, as the internationalist Menshevik Nikolai Sukhanov, who was opposed to the proposed insurrection, underlined with great lucidity in his memoirs: "What people needed were peace, bread, and land. They needed these things so much that unless they obtained them, they could no longer exist, and the state could no longer exist either. The people's needs were so great that everyone without exception, even the most savage peasant, understood them completely. The most savage peasant knew very well

that it was not in his power to satisfy these needs himself, and that the authorities would not grant them, for the authorities were evil, corrupt, and had to be destroyed. What could have been simpler or more logical?"

The situation encouraged the most vulgar form of demagoguery, Sukhanov added: "And the Bolsheviks, having overheated the atmosphere, followed this path. Their demagoguery was impudent and unrestrained. Not an iota of science, of the respect of principles, not a grain of the most elementary truth encumbered their discourse. They were all, from the modest agitator to the leaders themselves, to display exceptional qualities in this area."

Ironically, one of the crucial sessions of the Bolshevik Central Committee was held in Sukhanov's apartment, 32, Karpovka Street, #31, without his knowledge, of course, in early October. Among the participants were Lenin, Trotsky, Stalin, Sverdlov, Yakovleva, Lomov-Opokov, Kamenev, and Zinoviev. Kamenev and Zinoviev feared that, while it might be possible for the Bolsheviks to seize power with the insurrection, it would be difficult to keep it, in the context of economic difficulties and the distribution crisis. Nevertheless, a majority declared themselves in favor, and even set a date: October 15. The second pan-Russian Congress of the Soviets was to convene the same day (the Mensheviks would adjourn it on October 25).

The standoff between the two powers—Kerenski's government and the Soviet of Delegates—entered a new phase on October 12, with the inception of a revolutionary military committee by the Petrograd Soviet, at Trotsky's request. Henceforth, not only two governments, but also

A few minority groups excepted, public opinion was mostly hostile to the continuation of war against Germany. Here, in tragic irony, disabled veterans demonstrate in favor of the war. They are carrying a nationalist banner that reads: "Blind Veterans for War until Total Victory! Long Live Freedom!" Ph © L'Illustration/Sygma

The "Days of July" (July 3–14, 1917): Giving in to popular pressure, the Bolsheviks were forced to support a failed insurrection in Petrograd. Brutal repression ensued, along with a series of nationalist demonstrations, organized by the political right in numerous cities in Russia.
Ph © L'Illustration/Sygma

two armies, were facing each other, with both sides systematically revoking the orders of the other. The garrison of Petrograd was brought under the command of the Bolsheviks, and the Military Committee of the Revolution took immediate measures to prevent the evacuation of its troops.

The decision to act was taken on October 20, 1917. Trotsky's plan was implemented with extreme rapidity, in only a few days. During the night of October 24–25, the Red Guards seized strategic positions within the capital: the telephone operations center, the post offices, train stations, ministries, and the National Bank. Lenin was at the Bolshevik Party headquarters, in the Smolny Institute, where orders were dispatched. Kerenski, having exhausted all other alternatives, was forced to flee. On October 26, at 2:10 A.M., the soldiers of the revolution took control of the Winter Palace, the residence of the Romanoffs, and the ministers of the temporary government were arrested. A few hours later, the Soviet takeover was officially announced.

Peace, Land, and the Workers in Power

Since April 1917, the Bolsheviks had repeatedly declared that the Revolution, the end of hostilities followed by a democratic peace, and proletarian revolution in all of Europe, were inseparable aspects of a sole process. It is therefore no coincidence that the first decision of the new government of soldiers, workers, and peasants in the area of foreign affairs was to declare peace on October 26, 1917.

This decree had a rather original format for an official document in that it was an appeal to the peoples and governments of the world. This contained two contradictory lines of thinking. On the one hand, couched in the customary phrasing, it asked all the belligerent powers to open talks in view of a "just and democratic peace, desired by a huge majority of workers and working classes exhausted and martyrized by the war." In spite of its radical content, the language was that of international diplomacy and contained a proposal for an agreement based on the concession of mutual advantages. "An immediate peace, without annexations (in other words without conquest of foreign territory or peoples), and without the levy of reparations."

On the other hand, the decree addressed the "conscious workers" of the three most industrialized nations taking parting in the conflict: Great Britain, France and Germany were asked not only to "free humanity from the horrors of war and its consequences," but also to help

From the day of his return to Russia on April 2, 1917, Lenin rejected all collaboration with the temporary government. His rallying cry was: "All power to the Soviets!"

THE SOVNARKOM

On October 26, 1917, a "Council of Commissars of the People" (Sovnarkom) was designated to fulfill the role of a "temporary government of workers and peasants until the convening of a Constituent Assembly." It was made up of fifteen Commissars of the People: Vladimir Lenin (1870–1924), President of the Sovnarkom; Alexis Rykov (1881–1938), Interior Affairs; Vladimir Milyutin (1884–1937),

Agriculture; Alexander Chilapnikov (1885–1937), Labor; Vladimir Antonov-Ovseyenko (1883–1939), Nikolai Kirilenko (1885–1939), and Pavel Dybenko (1889–1938), Army and Navy; Victor Nogin (1878–1924), Industry and Trade; Anatoly Lunacharsky (1875–1933), Education; Ivan Skvorkov-Stepanov (1870–1928), Finance; Leo Trotsky (1879–1940), Foreign Affairs; George Lomov-Opokov

(1889–1938), Justice; I. A. Teodorovich (1875–1937), Logistics; Nikolai Glebov-Avilov (1887–1942), Mail and Telegraph; Joseph Stalin (1879–1953), Ethnic Affairs. Between November 1917 and January 1918, new ministries appeared, such as Social Services, headed by Alexandra Kollontai, (1872–1952). ∎

the government of the Soviets to conclude the process of "liberating the working masses from the yoke of slavery and exploitation." In this way, the proletariat of both warring sides, the Allied and the Central Powers, was integrated by the new government's decree into the history of the Revolution. Only the solidarity of the workers, imposing their will on their respective governments would ensure the victory of socialism in Russia. Interestingly, these workers were not asked to foment revolution in Europe, contrary to what the Bolsheviks had been saying in the previous months, and what they would say after peace was made.

Although the peace decree was important within the international context, the first genuinely deliberate legislation on the part of the Commissars of the People was the Land Decree, declared on the same day. Its ideological and linguistic structure was highly original; after all, it was conceived as the keystone of the new socialist state, meant to restore Russia's land to the people. In actuality, it simply gave a legal form to the agrarian revolution that the peasants had already accomplished in fact. It declared that the rights of the great landowners were abolished, and that Russian land was henceforth "placed at the disposal of the agrarian

LAND FOR THE PEASANTS

Extract of the "Peasants' Mandate on the Land," annexed to the Land Decree ratified by the Second Congress of the Soldiers' and Peasants' Soviet on October 26, 1917:
1) Private ownership of the land is abolished, and abolished forever. Land can no longer be bought or sold, rented or mortgaged, nor kept from the people in any way. All the land—whether it belongs to the state, to the Princes of the imperial family, to the Crown, to monasteries, to private persons, to peasants or peasant

committees, is hereby expropriated without indemnity, and is hereby bestowed upon the Russian people, and all those who till this land. To those who suffer damages from this transformation of property relationships, it is hereby recognized the right to certain assistance, for the period of time needed to adapt sufficiently to their new conditions of existence.
[...] 6) All citizens of the Russian state, male or female, possess the right to cultivate or work the land according to their desire, with the help of their families or in

cooperatives, and to the extent that they are competent and able to do so. Salaried labor is forbidden. In the event that any member of a rural community is rendered invalid and therefore unable to work, for the duration of two years, the community is bound to come to his aid by working his parcel collectively, until that member has recovered the capacity to work. Workers of the land who from old age or invalidity are definitively unable to work, lose the use of the land, but shall receive a state pension as compensation. ■

committees and the peasants' soviets of each district." It also gave the peasants' soviets the mandate to determine "the nature and size of the domains to be con-fiscated;... to maintain order during the process of expropriation of the largest landowners' property;... and to ensure the most

*F*rom left to right: Trotsky, Zinoviev, and Kamenev. Trotsky returned from exile on May 4, 1917, and joined the Bolsheviks. Soon elected president of the Petrograd Soviet, he would be the October Revolution's chief strategist. Zinoviev and Kamenev, members of the Bolshevik Party central committee, opposed igniting an armed insurrection, which they thought was premature.
Ph © L'Illustration/Sygma

vigorous defense of these lands that have become the property of the people." The task of finding a "definitive solution" to the transformation of privately owned land to a public regime was given to Constituent Assembly.

Following the February Revolution, the peasants had already started to seize unoccupied or fallow land, and to keep chopped wood and hay for themselves. They had forced many landowners to take flight in the course of countless revolts, and they had organized village, local, or district committees to ensure that seizures of larger domains were carried out legally. The Land Decree served to validate this spontaneous process. The nationalization of the land decreed by the Bolsheviks led to the concession of approximately 150 million hectares to the people. In the next two years, land appropriation continued without interruption, indeed at an accelerated pace, until, by March 1919, almost all of Russia's land was in the hands of the peasants.

The Bolsheviks were well aware of the dangers of this massive agrarian revolution on the socialist revolution as a whole. They knew that, in the peasants' view, the "devolvement of the land to the people" meant nothing less than that everyone should become a small landowner. This state of affairs was considered by the social democrats as a phenomenon integrally linked to the "dawn of a mature bourgeoisie," and that its acceptance implied acceptance of a bourgeois transition. But the Bolsheviks would not oppose the peasants' will. They thus created an alliance between the "rural revolt" and the "proletarian insurrection" that was to have a strategic importance during the civil war;

The Smolny Institute, an ancient high school for girls of the aristocracy, was the Bolshevik headquarters in Petrograd. It is here that the October Revolution was planned, down to the last details. Detachments of sailors, soldiers, and workers are posted around and inside the palace. From its first moments, the revolutionaries encountered very little resistance.
Ph © L'Illustration/Sygma

although there would be serious rifts due to the conflict between the urban proletariat and the peasants later on, the alliance would prevent the peasantry's interests from being captured by those of the "white" counter-revolution of aristocratic "White Russia," who had never accepted being dispossessed of their land.

It is remarkable that a revolution conceived and led by a party that presented itself as that of the workers had put the Land Decree at the top of the list of necessary legislation, thus giving strong validation to the general tendency toward occupation of the land. All the more so that, during the entire period of the democratic-bourgeois revolution, the workers' organizations had proved their vitality: they had penetrated ever further into the structures of production, and had already begun talking about workers managing the entire industrial apparatus themselves.

The factory committees, from March 1917 onward, stepped up their activity within the organizational structures and had obtained several economic advantages, notably the eight-hour day and a voice in production decisions, salaries, and layoffs. They had achieved several political advantages, too, such as the elimination

of sabotage by company directors of workers' strikes and the formation of a workers' militia. After October 25, the workers went into a mode of full-scale implementation of autonomous management of their workplaces.

There appeared an analogy between what was happening in the factories and on the farms. The peasants had demanded the expropriation of the great landowners and imposed the division of the land among those who had always cultivated it. Similarly, the workers, occupying their workplace and taking over production management collectively, demanded the expropriation of the factory owners and the right to manage the factories as a collective form of property. The Bolsheviks had supported this demand since the dawn of the revolutionary movement. But this was in contradiction with the social-democratic plan for development, which based itself on the view that modern capitalism was characterized by ever-increasing levels of concentration, and believed that the partition of the factories among the workers would bring the whole industrial apparatus back to a primitive level.

The workers' disillusion was not long in coming. The first measures passed by the revolutionary government

Inside the Winter Palace, before the revolutionary troops' assault, a thousand officer-cadets and a battalion of women prepared to defend the Kerenski government. On October 26, at 2:00 A.M., the Red Guards penetrated inside the ancient Imperial residence. The Soviet takeover was declared at 5:00 A.M.

Ph © L'Illustration/Sygma

Moscow, October 1917: Dismantling a Czarist monument. During the Days of October, when the Bolshevik press "denounced" acts of vandalism against historic buildings, everyone was talking about the destruction of St. Basil's Cathedral—a false rumor that shows the level of misinformation. The Commissar for Education, Anatoly Lunacharsky, called on the population to "defend Russian cultural traditions." In fact, damage to the symbols of the former regime was extremely limited.
Ph © L'Illustration/Sygma

dealt with satisfying the demands of the soldiers, sailors, and the Red Guard of Petrograd. In particular, priority was given to them in the distribution of rations and supplies, for the city of Petrograd was overrun by deserters from the front, many of whom were starving.

On November 18, for example, the Sovnarkom announced the increase of food rations for soldiers, and eliminated differences in soldiers' and officers' diets. The deliberations on the subject of the workers were surprisingly moderate and cautious, aside from the decree on the eight-hour day (October 29, 1917), and the decree on workers' control of production. The latter, promulgated late (November 14, 1917), provoked general discontent. It laid out the new tasks and obligations of the state as CEO and encouraged worker participation in affairs concerning the workplace, but it also fixed the limits of this type of self-management. The response of the workers was to demand the equality of wages and the abolition of piecework, and to continue their occupation of the factories, of which they judged themselves the rightful owners.

A new difficulty arose when it came time to face the

issue of nationalization. Tensions were bound to become exacerbated among the workers in "socialized" factories, as the writer Alexander Lozovski, future director of the International Communist Union, noted: "The factory committee will not be able to escape fusion with the administration. For the masses of workers, the committee and the administration will be interchangeable. All requests that were previously addressed to the administration will now be addressed to the committees. Under the threat of a strike, the committee will have to accede to their demands. Once they control the factories, the committees will no longer be able to tell the workers that they are unable to raise the minimum wage an unlimited number of times."

Wage demands quickly took on the allure of an epidemic, to which no member of the proletariat displayed any immunity. The working masses began feverishly to seek out what the Commissar of Labor, Alexander Shlyapnikov, in a recent appeal to the workers, called the "superfluous paper ruble." Faced with the spreading strikes, the government ordered all factories in Petrograd to be shut down on December 23, validating the state of unrest of the proletariat of the Revolution's capital city. Indeed, in the factories of Petrograd, appeals for calm and discipline went largely unheeded, and unions were boycotted everywhere, since they were now

THE DISSOLUTION OF THE CONSTITUENT ASSEMBLY

The consolidation of the Bolsheviks' hold on power was achieved through this radical act. The Constituent Assembly was a representative body whose mission, during the transition from an old political form to a new, was to elaborate a constitution for the new Russia. The temporary government had postponed convening the Assembly until November 12, 1917. After the takeover, the Bolsheviks, who had already committed themselves to the principle as far back as their 1903 platform, delivered on their promise. But the results of the elections of November–December 1917 were disappointing. Out of 707 elected representatives, there were 370 revolutionary socialists and 40 radical revolutionaries, while the Bolsheviks obtained only 170 seats, with members of various national groups taking 86, the cadets 17, and the Mensheviks 16.

The government of the Commissars of the People responded by deciding to deny any autonomous body of authority. The Constituent Assembly convened on January 5, 1918, but it was immediately dissolved by a decree of the Executive Committee of the Soviets. The new constitution of the Russian state would never be the result of an equilibrium between the political forces in play, as the Constituent Assembly was supposed to embody. ∎

Red Square: Patriotic demonstration and review of troops during the Revolution. Fighting was far fiercer in Moscow than in Petrograd, where several thousand fell victim to the violence, which lasted several days. On the dawn of November 3, all of Moscow was in revolutionary hands.
Ph © L'Illustration/Sygma

seen as little more than new bosses. Pamphlets calling for the "dismantling and the defeat of the workers' organizations" circulated among the workers of the capital: "The unions appeal to our self-control and our conscience. But they are throwing us into the hands of even more numerous exploiters. They are not workers', but bosses' organizations. We must declare war on them, boycott them. Not a kopeck shall be paid to the unions, nor to the parties, nor to the Soviets." Acts of violence were recorded against members of factory

administrations; sometimes the victims were the workers' own comrades in the elected committees. Some administrators were unceremoniously placed in wheelbarrows to be thrown out of the factories.

Chapter 3

FROM **T**REATY TO **C**IVIL **W**AR

AN ILLUSION OF PEACE AFTER THE SIGNING OF AN ARMISTICE WITH GERMANY IS SOON SHATTERED. THE NEW REGIME HAS TO FACE A COUNTERREVOLUTIONARY ARMY AND THE ISSUE OF NATIONAL DIVERSITY—IN THE UKRAINE AND ELSEWHERE.

While the Days of February were making the front pages of every major newspaper in Europe, bourgeois readers tried to minimize the importance of the event, which in their view was a result of the breakdown in the communications and transportation networks. In the beginning, the working classes retained the fact that the workers were against the war. From February, when instead of playing watchdog to the temporary government, the Bolsheviks began to exercise parallel government, it became clear that socialism had a hopeful future, and soon there was considerable enthusiasm. But the October Revolution had little initial impact on people's minds. Few believed in the capacity of the Russian proletariat to spearhead a worldwide revolution. In France, no one realized that a new chapter in history was being written. In Italy, perhaps more than elsewhere, people seem to have understood the importance of the devolution of power to the workers and the peasants.

Politicians all over Europe, however, knew what was going on. They knew also that their own citizens, engaged in the war effort, might feel inclined to respond to the Bolsheviks' appeal to join in the anti-war protest and, through strikes and demonstrations, considerably destabilize the situation, in spite of the difficulty in communicating with Russia, and the strict censorship

The counterrevolution was being organized almost simultaneously with the Soviet takeover. Anti-Bolshevik resistance was initially defeated in Moscow, Petrograd, and within the army; it took a stronger and more radical hold in the south of Russia, especially in the Cossack regions of the Don River and Kuban. With foreign military intervention on the side of the counterrevolutionaries, the conflict quickly escalated to full-fledged war. The Allied Powers feared the spread of Bolshevism in Europe, and by the second half of 1918, they were actively supporting the White Russian Army.
Ph © L'Illustration/Sygma

of battle developments enforced by the military. The authorities' response was on the whole an obdurate silence. Nevertheless, the pacifist propaganda of the Bolsheviks had considerable appeal, and not only to proletarians or revolutionaries. Jacques Sadoul, a member of the French military contingent in Russia, observed: "Revolution is peace. And it is therefore wrongfully that people compare the heroic French armies of the Revolution of 1793 with the helpless Russian troops of 1917. In 1793, Revolution produced war; in 1917, war produced the Revolution."

This link between revolution and peace was also vividly rendered by another French officer in Petrograd, Pierre Pascal, on October 30, 1917: "This morning, huge peace demonstration. An extraordinary expression of the will of the people: everything is in perfect order, the regiments with their leaders—wearing no epaulettes or other signs of rank; men on horseback, individuals marching peacefully and calmly. Many banners. A few officers are recognizable. Workers. Armed Red Guards. Women. Little chanting. This is the strength of a people passing in the street, marching toward a pure ideal of justice and of good. Tears were in my eyes watching them."

The lubok is a kind of popular print in Russia, usually accompanied by a short explanatory note. The text of this anti-German lubok from 1914–15 by Kasimir Malevich reads: "Look over there, by the Vistula River! The Germans have a tummy ache, things are going sour!"
Ph © BDIC/D.R.

The Illusion of Peace

Of course, the People's Commissars' first decrees created a sensation. The order for Russian soldiers to fraternize with the enemy, the proposal to the Germans for a cessation of hostilities, the refusal to honor financial obligations contracted by the Czar abroad, the publication of old secret treaties between the Russians and the Allied Powers—these acts broke all the rules of traditional diplomacy. Soon, fear of revolution gripped the ruling classes of Europe, who were united in their adamant opposition to the idea that Russian Bolsheviks could foment unrest in their own countries. They understood the need to shatter the myth of a state controlled by workers and peasants, to eliminate this *coup d'état* that had benefited from the dereliction of the Czarist regime. The Western powers did not delay in contacting White Russian forces, which were already organizing their counter-offensive.

With the Peace Decree, the new regime had proposed that the warring sides sign an armistice and open

negotiations for peace. But the Allies threatened serious reprisals in the event that the Treaty of September 5, 1914 binding the Allied powers was to be unilaterally violated. Their intransigence led the Bolsheviks to start talks separately with Germany, which, with recent developments in the war, had a strong interest in having one less front to manage. On December 3, 1917, an armistice was signed, followed on March 3, 1918 by the Treaty of Brest-Litovsk.

True, the Bolsheviks had to overcome opposition from its most internationalist faction, the "left-wing communists," calling for a revolutionary war against Germany. But they succeeded in ratifying the peace. The Treaty of Brest-Litovsk imposed draconian conditions on

Anti-German lubok from 1914–15 by the poet Vladimir Mayakovsky. Left: "At Warsaw and Grodnow, we beat the Germans as hard as we could"; right: "Even our women will kill cockroaches" (pun on proussak, *which means both cockroach and Prussian).*
Ph © BDIC/D.R.

Russia: what was ratified was in effect the dissolution of the Russian Empire. Russia was forced to cede to the enemy vast and fertile regions by recognizing the Ukraine's independence; it also lost Finland, most of Belarus, and parts of the Caucasus, and had to renounce its territorial pretensions in the Baltic and in Poland. Six million marks were paid to the Germans as war reparations.

It was quite a paradoxical situation. On the one hand, the Soviet government was openly sponsoring agitation

Peace negotiations opened on December 9, 1917 at Brest-Litovsk. Here, the Soviet delegates, Ambassador Joffé and Leo Kamenev, are received by the German generals. The Treaty of Brest-Litovsk was signed on March 3, 1918, to Russia's great disadvantage. It would be annulled by the Soviet government after the armistice of November 13, 1918, sanctioning German defeat.
Ph © L'Illustration/Sygma

among the working class in Berlin through its Ambassador, Adolphe Joffé, with the aim of fomenting a revolution in Germany—considered by the Bolsheviks as the prelude to a worldwide revolution. On the other, the German governments' representatives in Moscow, led by Ambassador the Viscount Wilhelm von Mirbach, were doing their best to help the Bolshevik revolution to the extent that they were disorganizing the Allied Powers' war machine. Of course, the Allied Powers were themselves busy fanning the flames of the counterrevolutionary front within Russia.

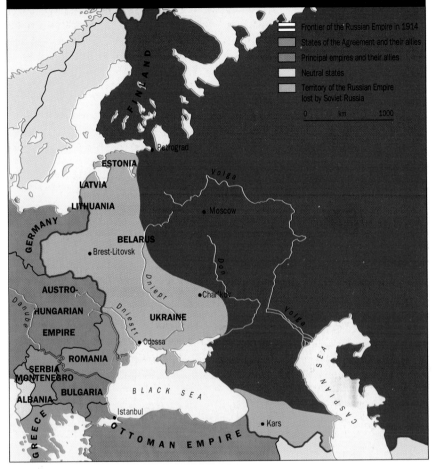

THE TREATY OF BREST-LITOVSK

Frontier of the Russian Empire in 1914
States of the Agreement and their allies
Principal empires and their allies
Neutral states
Territory of the Russian Empire lost by Soviet Russia

0   km   1000

FINLAND

Petrograd

ESTONIA
LATVIA
LITHUANIA

GERMANY

BELARUS

Brest-Litovsk

Volga

Moscow

Don

Dniepr

Volga

AUSTRO-
HUNGARIAN
EMPIRE

Danube

Dniestr

UKRAINE

Charkov

Odessa

CASPIAN SEA

ROMANIA
SERBIA
MONTENEGRO
BULGARIA
ALBANIA

GREECE

BLACK SEA

Istanbul

OTTOMAN EMPIRE

Kars

A "Besieged Fortress"

The Bolsheviks were fully aware that the Revolution's survival was dependent upon resolving the military issue. With the Peace Decree, the negotiations, and then the treaty signed at Brest-Litovsk, it attempted to end a bloody and unpopular war. But the respite was not to last. A terrible civil war was brewing, which would claim millions of lives. The entire country would become the theater of massacres, battles, famine, and epidemics, which would lay waste to the land and the people, economically and socially.

The Cossacks were the first to organize a military

The Treaty of Brest-Litovsk forced Russia to cede Poland, the Baltic States, part of Belarus, and the Caucasus. It also recognized the independence of Finland and the Ukraine.

opposition to the new regime. Descendants of colonists settled in the fifteenth century at the confines of the empire, the Cossacks had become during the nineteenth century one of the pillars of the autocracy. The radical hostility the Cossacks displayed toward the Bolsheviks was above all the result of the governmental decree that abolished all class distinctions and all hierarchies, thus depriving the Cossacks of their social status.

In 1917, there were thirteen Cossack armies spread out all over Russia (out of a population of 4.5 million). Over 53 million hectares of land were under their control, most of which was managed collectively by the village communities, or *stanitsy*. The very day of the Revolution, October 25, 1917, Alexis Kaledin, chief of the Cossacks (*ataman*), declared an independent Cossack government in the Don River region, soon followed by the *atamans* of the Kuban region (A.P. Filimonov), of Orenburg (Alexander Dutov), and of Ussuri (Grigori Semyenov), who organized anti-Bolshevik formations. These groupings were often ethnically heterogeneous: For example, Semyenov's army, which engaged the Red Army to the east of Lake Baikal, near Manchuria, was made up of Chinese,

Mongols, Buriats, Serbs, and Cossacks from the trans-Baikal region.

Meanwhile, the leaders of the Bolsheviks' Russian enemies were regrouping in the frontier areas of the southern provinces, forming a volunteer army with the Cossacks. Around this core, the "White Army" came into being under the command of Lavr Kornilov (December 25, 1917–April 13, 1918), then Anton Denikin (April 13, 1918–January 8, 1919).

The first concerted offensive against the Bolsheviks took place in May 1918, along the Trans-Siberian railroad. The Czechoslovak legion, a powerful regiment composed of about 30,000 men and officers, had surrendered after having fought alongside the Austro-Hungarian army. The Allies had already negotiated their evacuation through Vladivostok. Suddenly, there was a change of plans. Abetted by the Allies, the legion proclaimed itself opposed to the Bolsheviks and began to overrun a series of strategic positions. The legionnaires reached the Volga. From there, Cheliabinsk, Penza, Tomsk, Omsk, Samara, Krasnoyarsk, Vladivostok, Simbirsk, Ekaterinenburg, and Kazan fell in rapid succession to the rogue regiment. Siberia's vast territory was soon wrested

Charge of the Cossack cavalry. During the entire civil war, the Cossacks showed an ambivalent attitude. After October, they favored the idea of regional autonomy. Hostile to the Communists, they remained aloof from the Russian bourgeoisie's idea of national patriotism, and also from the prospect of a restored ancien régime.
Ph © L'Illustration/Sygma

from Bolshevik control.

At the same time, Japanese and American troops, as well as small English, French, and Italian units debarked at Vladivostok, under the pretext of coming to the aid of the Czech regiment. The situation was becoming more and more confused, with anti-Bolshevik entities sprouting up in Siberia and in the eastern provinces of European Russia. (Provisional govern-

1917 AND WESTERN MARXISTS

The October Revolution was the culminating point of a long debate about power among Russian and European social democrats. In Germany, Karl Kautsky (1854–1938) vituperated the Bolshevik regime and the dictatorship of the proletariat. He never abandoned his conviction that Russia was not ripe for a socialist revolution because it did not meet the requirements for socialism to succeed: that is, a strong, proletariat a sufficient level of democracy, and a highly developed industrial base. For others, the Revolution provoked doubt and intense soul-searching as to what social democracy should be and a rereading of Marx's works. The Italian theoretician, Antonio Gramsci (1891-1937) found in Russian events a new perspective on Marx, a way to filter out the positivism and naturalism that encumbered Marx's thinking. The Revolution was not just a mechanical consequence of economic factors:

"The Bolsheviks' Revolution was a revolution against Marx's *Capital*.

Capital was much more the book of the bourgeoisie than of the proletariat. It was the critical demonstration of the necessary formation in Russia of a bourgeoisie, the necessary rise of capitalism, of Western-style civilization, before the proletariat could begin to dream about its own revolt, its needs, and its revolution. But the facts went much further than any ideology. The events disproved, indeed they annihilated, the theoretical framework of the ideal revolution, which sought to have Russian history follow the principles of historical materialism. The Bolsheviks negated Karl Marx. Their direct action and the conquest they achieved showed that historical materialism was far more flexible than people expected it could be. There was a certain fatality in these events, and although the Bolsheviks disowned some of *Capital*'s theses, they never disowned the essence of Marx's powerful ideas. They weren't simply Marxists, they hadn't written up a doctrine, with dogmatic and undeniable assertions. They

experienced true Marxism, the immortal product of German and Italian idealism, with all its positivist and naturalist incrustations. This thinking never places raw economic realities at the center of history, but instead man himself, and society, interactions and understanding that develop in civilization, and collective desires. And will, which understands economic reality, evaluates it, adapts it to its needs, becomes the motor of the economy, the true author of objective reality. A living, moving reality, much like molten lava, that can be channeled to the extent and in the direction that this will allows it to go."

Antonio Gramsci, "The Revolution against *Capital*" *Avanti!* 24 November 1917. ∎

ments were set up at Samara, Omsk, Arkhangelsk, Ural, Turkestan, Crimea, and ethnically-based governments were established in the Cossack, Turko-Tatar, and Bashkir provinces, as well as Cossack military governments, among others).

By the end of August, no fewer than 30 governments were in operation all over the former Czarist Empire. The most influential among them was the Constituent

Committee of Samara (*komutch*). Formed on June 8, 1918 and benefiting from the protection of the Czech legion, its leaders were all ex-members of the defunct national Constituent Assembly (revolutionary socialists I. Brouchvit, B. Fortunatov, V. Volski, and I. Nesterov). During its brief tenure, it implemented land nationalization and expropriations from landowners, but it also abolished the concept of workers' authority and nationalization of businesses encouraged by the Bolsheviks—in sum it was an alternative to the Bolshevik revolution. The Samara Committee was as much opposed to the idea of a restored monarchy as it was to socialist experimentation, looking rather

*L*enin surrounded by a group of military leaders, in Red Square, May 1919. In this crucial year of the civil war, the White Armies concentrated their forces on revolutionary Russia. The Red Army would succeed in vanquishing its adversaries, one after the other.
Ph © Keystone

In August 1917, General Kornilov had failed in his attempt to install a military government in Petrograd. After the Bolshevik Revolution, with an army of volunteers, he would join the civic Soviet of the Don, one of the first counterrevolutionary organizations. He died in combat at Ekaterinodar in March 1918.
Ph © L'Illustration/Sygma

toward a parliamentary democracy centered upon agrarian reform. Its principal competitor was the regional government of Siberia, headquartered in Omsk and master of a huge swath of territory, with Cheliabinsk at the other end.

At the Conference of Oufa (September 8–23, 1918), these governments made an attempt to put together an anti-Bolshevik authority that had the legitimacy to oppose the government of the Soviets. At its convening there were 170 delegates—most of them socialist revolutionaries, representatives of different governments, and parties and organizations sharing a common hostility to the Bolsheviks. After two weeks of debates, a compromise was finally struck between two different styles of government: democratic and parliamentary on the one hand, and reactionary and authoritarian on the other. On September 23, the conference declared the inception of a temporary "pan-Russian" government, based in Omsk, pending the convening of a constituent assembly. Five men made up the directorate: Nikolai Avskentiev (right-wing revolutionary socialist, leader of the Komutch), N.I. Astrov (cadet party), Vassily Boldirev (liberal), Piotr Vologodski (liberal, president of the government of Siberia), and Nikolai Tchaikovsky (popular socialist, president of the government of the northern province). In its program, the directorate envisioned the destruction of the Soviet regime, continuing the war against Germany according to valid treaties, recovering territory Russia had lost, creating a national army and a democratic regime, and finally annulling debts contracted by the Bolsheviks.

But during the night of November 18, 1919, the

directorate was overthrown by Admiral Alexander Kolchak with the help of the British, whose supreme authority in Russia was recognized by the counter-revolutionary generals and the Allied Powers alike. There were now two fronts in the civil war: in the South, along the edge of the steppe, were General Denikin's army, and in the East, territory east of the Volga was under General Kolchak's control.

The behavior of the Allied Powers, which supported the counter-revolutionary movement, was to play an important role in the war's progressive escalation. Initially, although they adopted a hostile stance vis-à-vis the Bolshevik government, the prevailing mood was patience. They were mostly preoccupied with halting the German advance on the Eastern front, and preventing the transfer of troops west. This led to the English forces debarking at Murmansk in March 1918, and to the arrival of Japanese troops at Vladivostok in early April, followed by an American contingent. Quickly, foreign intervention took on an overtly anti-Bolshevik tone, with the Allied Powers supplying military, economic, and political aid to the counter-revolutionaries.

There were several factors influencing this strategy. First, Russia's unilateral exit from the war considerably jeopardized the military strength of the Allies. Then there were the consequences of the Bolsheviks' measures: the annulment of Czarist debts with foreign powers, the nationalization of the Russian industry, in large part owned and operated by foreign capital, and the confiscation of the stock assets of private banks by the State bank. This seriously hurt the economic interests of industrialists and international financiers. Of course,

On April 4, 1920, General Piotr Wrangel succeeds Anton Denikin as the head of the White Army. Headquartered in the Crimea, he launched numerous successful raids against the Bolsheviks in the southern provinces and arrived at Ekaterinoslav, where he set up a new government. He was finally defeated in 1920 and forced into exile.
Ph © L'Illustration/Sygma

In Siberia, Admiral Alexander Kolchak assembled an anti-Bolshevik army, supported by the Allied Powers. In 1918–19, his troops were the principal threat to the Soviet regime. But after defeat at Samara (April 1919) and the occupation of Omsk by the Red Army (November 1919), the Admiral took flight. Captured by the Bolsheviks, he was executed.
Ph © L'Illustration/Sygma

there was also considerable debate about whether or not to intervene directly in Russia's affairs. On July 17, 1918, the American Secretary of State spoke in a communiqué addressed to the Allied ambassadors: "The United States government, after a long and detailed examination of the situation in Russia, has seen fit to say its final word on the subject: a military intervention would only increase the confusion in Russia, instead of remedying it. It would harm Russia instead of helping it, and would in no way bring us closer to our objective, which is winning the war against Germany. In consequence, the United States of America will neither participate in this intervention nor condone it."

In fact, during the summer of 1918, Allied debarkations in Russia intensified. In August, an Anglo-Canadian contingent arrived in the Trans-Caucasus and occupied Baku, while the French and English overthrew the local government at Arkangelsk. In Odessa, French troops offered to join Denikin's army, committed in the Don region. With the end of the World War in November, the Allied Powers abandoned all hesitation and clearly revealed their hostility to the Communists. The fear of revolution spreading to Central Europe had united different interests, and Russia was soon to find itself surrounded by a veritable buffer zone. The results were immediate: Russia lost vast territories and huge amounts of raw materials and combustible resources, it was isolated within the international community by an economic blockade, and it lost the entirety of its foreign trade.

In 1919, Kolchak launched an offensive toward the Volga River, fanning out his troops in a wide front. But after a few victories, he was unable to coordinate his movements with those of Denikin's army and was forced to retreat—nor did he succeed in rejoining the forces that the Allied Powers had displaced in the far north of the country. The advance of the Red Army led to the disintegration of Kolchak's forces. On November 10,

1919, Omsk was evacuated and taken a few days later by the Bolsheviks. Kolchak retreated to Irkutsk, where a revolt broke out on Christmas Eve. On January 20, 1920, his government was definitively dissolved. Admiral Kolchak was arrested and executed by a firing squad in the environs of Irkutsk in March 1920. On the eastern front, the Czech legion was evacuated, the French and English contingents retreated, and the Japanese were left alone to face the Bolsheviks.

After the fall of Kolchak, General Denikin took over the supreme authority of the counterrevolutionary movement. He had already taken over much of the Ukraine, beating out the armies of his nationalist rival Simon Petlyura. In the summer of 1919, he launched an offensive on Moscow, with General Nikolai Yudenich's troops reinforcing his own from the northwest. Denikin was soon roughly 250 miles from the capital, while Iudenich had arrived at the gates of Petrograd, when an unexpected counteroffensive by the Red Army chased Denikin and his men all the way to Crimea. Finally defeated in early 1920, he was forced to cede command to Baron Piotr von Wrangel.

The counterrevolutionary generals: Nikolai Yudenich (left) and Anton Denikin (right). The final defeat of the White Russians was not only military, for the class struggle ended up taking precedence in the civil war. In the rear of the counterrevolutionary front, there were peasant and worker uprisings, and an organized resistance led by Bolshevik partisan brigades.
Ph © L'Illustration/Sygma

Russian soldiers of the White Army, in tatters. In the beginning, the average peasant sympathized with the counterrevolutionary cause—especially once the Bolsheviks had starting requisitioning their wheat. But the Whites would quickly alienate the rural population by their ambition to reestablish the landed domains.

Ph © L'Illustration/Sygma

The Nationalities: The Case of the Ukraine

To understand the civil war, one must understand the ethnic diversity of Russia. The Russian Empire was huge and included people of many ethnicities, whose languages were often totally unrelated. In the West, there were European peoples, belonging to the European sphere of culture; their level of development was comparable to their Western neighbors. On the contrary the Eastern peoples were far closer, culturally and materially, to Asia. There, the relationship between the central administration and the local population had remained essentially colonial.

Slavs formed the majority of the population of Russia—65 percent—and were divided in three distinct families, almost three distinct nationalities, in fact: 75 million Great-Russians or Muscovites (43.8 percent), 30 million Lesser-Russians or Ukrainians (17.6 percent), 8 million White Russians (4.6 percent), totaling 113 million out of a population of 170 million. In the southeast, Georgia and Armenia excepted, there was far less ethnic, linguistic, or political cohesion. The

THE RESISTANCE OF THE "GREENS"

During the civil war, the word *zhelienye* (green) designated all those who fled conscription by hiding in the forest, especially in the northern Caucasus and in the Crimea.

After the general mobilization decreed by Denikin in southern Russia in the summer of 1918, hundreds of workers and peasants left their villages in Tchernomoria and the factories of Novorossisk to take refuge in the nearby mountains. Nearly all were veterans who refused to return to war. But these deserters soon had to, for the White Army pursued them relentlessly and persecuted their families. The repression certainly led to the return of a few of them and their conscription into the White Army; most, however, chose to organize their own defensive force against these punitive actions. From small groups of five or six men dispersed in the wilds, added men and weapons would produce a veritable partisan militia, actively supported by the civil population. The Green movement was at its height from the end of 1919 to 1920, along the Caucasian coast of the Black Sea, at the same time as Denikin's army was starting to disintegrate. It is also worth noting that many of the Greens had effectively deserted from the Red Army.

The actual effect of the Green army on the war was almost negligible, for the partisans had no impact on the general development of the civil war. But having this form of agitation going on in the rear was bad for Denikin's morale and that of his troops. Indeed, irrational fears spread about the "secret and invisible" Greens. The Greens did enjoy great freedom of movement in the Black Sea region, and crossed enemy lines with ease. Denikin's men imagined them to be everywhere, in each village, behind every bush, in the streets of Novorossisk, and even within their own ranks.

The Green army had no unified or compact organization, however. In spite of a certain common goal, there was never any concerted decision-making, logistical or otherwise, and no common reserves of supplies. Neither were they politically homogeneous, for all tendencies were represented, from Bolsheviks in the zone between Novorossisk and Gelendzik, socialist revolutionaries in the area south of Gelendzik, and other groups composed of peasants in the Tuaps region whose only goal was to defend themselves against pillage by the White Army. The socialist revolutionary

influence was quite strong, especially around Sotchi, where a Committee for the Liberation of the Black Sea was created, which established power over the region, even entering talks with the Menshevik authorities of Georgia, and printing its own currency. ■

Spring, 1918: Red Army recruitment of workers in Moscow. On May 29, 1918, the Bolshevik government published a decree of general mobilization.
Ph © Keystone

cultural and material state of these regions was in many areas extremely backward.

When the Bolsheviks took power, the Empire they inherited from the temporary government was about to disintegrate following the military debacle and the social unrest fomented by those in power locally. Central authority was very weak and did not effectively extend beyond the central and southern provinces of Russia. These areas were to rally to the revolution relatively

Refugees and White Army volunteers evacuate Odessa, fleeing the advance of the Red Army. The city was taken on February 8, 1920, after Denikin's defeat.

Ph © L'Illustration/Sygma

quickly and easily. But it took many months for the Communists' influence to reach south to the Ukraine and east to Siberia. Even then, this was rather more due to former feelings of unity and dependence. The Treaty of Brest-Litovsk had taken a large amount of western territory away from Russia, and the Civil War would deeply divide the country. At one point, the Republic of the Soviets' influence was reduced to a zone roughly corresponding to the former Principality of Moscow. The Bolsheviks absolutely had to recover the boundaries of the former empire, and the people in these territories—in the name of the Revolution.

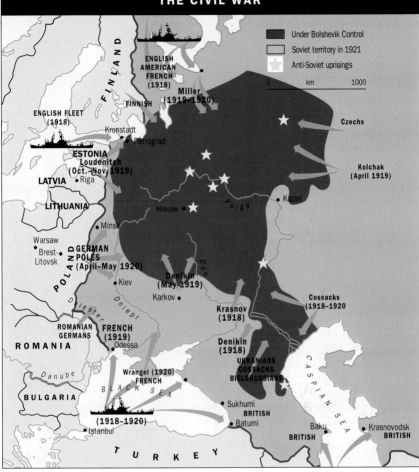

THE CIVIL WAR

Legend:
- Under Bolshevik Control
- Soviet territory in 1921
- Anti-Soviet uprisings

0   km   1000

FINLAND

ENGLISH
AMERICAN
FRENCH
(1918)

Miller
(1919–1920)

FINNISH

Czechs

ENGLISH FLEET
(1918)

Kronstadt
Petrograd

ESTONIA
Loudenitch
(Oct.–Nov. 1919)

LATVIA · Riga

LITHUANIA

Kolchak
(April 1919)

Moscow

Volga

Kazan

· Minsk

Warsaw
Brest-
Litovsk

GERMAN
POLES
(April–May 1920)

POLAND

Dniester

Dniepr

· Kiev

Denikin
(May 1919)

Karkov ·

Don

Krasnov
(1918)

Cossacks
(1918–1920)

ROMANIAN
GERMANS

FRENCH
(1919)
Odessa

ROMANIA

Denikin
(1918)

CASPIAN SEA

Danube

Wrangel (1920)
FRENCH

UKRANIANS
COSSACKS
BIELORUSSIANS

BULGARIA

BLACK SEA

(1918–1920)

· Istanbul

· Sukhumi

BRITISH
· Batumi

Baku

· Krasnovodsk
BRITISH

BRITISH

T U R K E Y

The Soviet government had to decide whether to accept the secession of peoples desiring independence, organize a federation of peoples with varying levels of autonomy, or impose the total incorporation of the territories and people in a new kind of state. The path that was taken reflected an idea Lenin had first voiced in 1916: nationalism had a revolutionary value that should be encouraged and exploited and finally transformed into socialism. The Declaration of the Rights of the Peoples of Russia (November 2, 1917) expressed four principles: equality and sovereignty of all the peoples of Russia; the right to self-determination,

Simon Petlyura, former Minister of War in the first independent Ukrainian government, is head of the Ukrainian nationalist movement. The civil war traumatized this nation more than any other in the former empire. In the Ukraine, there were fourteen governments in four years.

Ph © L'Illustration/Sygma

including secession and the creation of an independent state; suppression of all national or religious restrictions and privileges; and free development of national minorities and ethnic groups over the entire Russian territory.

On the western frontier, this policy would lead, before the end of 1920, to the recognition of independent republics in Poland, Finland, Lithuania, Latvia, and Estonia, as well as the installation of Soviet republics in the Ukraine and Belarus, very close to the Russian Soviet Republic. Toward the east, a different pattern emerged, due to the particular course the Civil War took in these regions, with alliances forged between the counterrevolutionaries and Asian peoples. In eastern Siberia, a buffer state was set up: the Independent Democratic Republic of the Far East (April 6, 1920, recognized by the Soviet government a month later).

The most emblematic case was that of the Ukraine. Possessing one of the most fertile soils in the world, the Ukraine, with its superabundant wealth of grains, vegetables, and fruits, had long been known as the pantry of Europe. Over the centuries, control of the Ukraine had been hotly contested by the Turks, the Germans, the Poles, and imperial Russia, which had finally won the prize. After the February Revolution, the Ukrainian bourgeoisie immediately brought up the issue of independence. In March 1917, the youth nationalist movement organized a central soviet or Rada (council in Ukrainian), which, shortly after the October Revolution, proclaimed an independent popular republic. On December 4, 1917, the Soviet government addressed a declaration to the Rada recognizing the republic on the basis of the right to self-determination, but also accusing its authorities of denying the power of the local soviets.

In fact, the Communist Party had not attained a high level of organization in the region. At the Congress of Soviets at Kiev on December 3, the Bolsheviks were outnumbered by partisans of the Rada. A new Ukrainian Congress was convened on December 11 at Karkov, which resulted in an executive committee composed of Bolsheviks and other left-wing socialist revolutionaries. The Soviets' policy in response was double-barreled: recognizing the executive committee as the legitimate authority in the Ukraine, they also opened talks with the Rada, members of which participated in the negotiations of Brest-Litovsk.

On January 9, 1918, the Rada proclaimed the Ukrainian Republic a sovereign state. The German government recognized it immediately. The Red Army, however, had surrounded Kiev, and on January 26 entered the city. The Rada was overthrown and replaced by a new Soviet Ukrainian government, which lasted three weeks. Meanwhile, Rada delegates took part in the treaty negotiations, along with a communist Ukrainian delegation, to which they were opposed. In late January, a separate treaty was signed with the Germans.

A MINISTRY OF NATIONALITIES

The Russian Empire had been formed by the successive annexation of territories belonging to vastly different cultural spheres. In 1917, this "Prison of Peoples" exploded. The creation of a ministry the likes of which Russia had never seen, the Commissariat of National Affairs, reflects the importance Bolsheviks gave to the resolution of this issue. The new ministry was led by Joseph Vissarionovich Djugachvili, aka Stalin (1879–1953). Since his joining the Central Committee of the Bolshevik Party in 1912, Stalin had endeavored to define the relationship between Marxism and the national question. His first mission as People's Commissar was to go to Helsinki in 1917, to communicate to the Finnish Social Democratic Party the Soviets' intention to recognize Finland's right to self-determination. A month later, he passed a decree establishing the country's independence. In fact, Stalin's mission was to preserve the unity of the former empire, within a new structure that was to be called the Union of Soviet Socialist Republics (USSR). The Commissariat of National Affairs (Narkomnats) would serve as a centralizing organization through which Stalin worked toward obtaining the non-Russian nations' collaboration and allegiance to Moscow. The Constitution of 1918 stipulates a form of federalism founded on the unity of national territories and guaranteeing regional autonomy to all territorial units with a specific ethnic coherence. ■

On February 12, the delegates asked the Germans to invade the Ukraine, who promptly complied. The Bolsheviks were forced to leave Kiev, which was retaken by a Ukrainian nationalist, Simon Petlyura. The Rada was quickly sidelined from power, and on April 29, it was replaced by a reactionary government installed by the Germans under the command of General Pavel Skoropadski, whose program was to restore the landowners and prevent any social reform.

Mikhail Hrushevski, a historian, president of the Rada, surrounded here by Ukrainian Ministers. Ardent partisan of independence, Krushevsi took over the National Council in 1917. Exiled in 1919, he would recognize the Soviet government five years later. He was then allowed to return to Kiev, and resume his academic career.
Ph © L'Illustration/Sygma

He would remain in power until November 14, 1918, when, faced with the capitulation of the German occupying troops, the Rada was replaced by a "Ukrainian Directorate" presided over by Vladimir Vinichenko, under the military command of Simon Petlyura. From January to February 1919, the Red Army launched an offensive, successively conquering Karkov, Poltava, Ekaterinoslav, and Live. In March, Soviet troops took over Kerson and Nikolayev, and in April, Odessa, Sebastopol, and Simferopol, all with the approval of the vast majority of civilians. The Directorate sought in vain the support of the Allied Powers (in particular France), but their preoccupation was far more with the fate of the White Army than that of nationalist movements.

At this point, three sets of forces were in the Ukrainian arena. The Bolsheviks had established their capital at Karkov, one of the biggest industrial centers in the region, with a Soviet Socialist Republic founded on March 10, 1919. Petlyura's troops, guilty among other things of terrible pogroms against the sizeable Jewish community, were massed in the west. In the

MAKHNO, THE ANARCHIST COSSACK

Nestor Makhno (1889–1934) became a living legend in the Ukraine. From 1918–1921, he headed a powerful peasant army that successively fought against the Directorate, Denikin, Wrangel, and the Bolsheviks. On several occasions he composed temporary alliances with the Communists against the common White Russian enemy, but he always opposed attempts to install a soviet government in the Ukraine. In August 1921, he was forced to take refuge in Romania. The following is an extract from a Makhnovist tract:

"Why are we called Makhnovists? Because we have seen appear among us, in the darkest days of the reaction in the Ukraine, our trusty friend and guide Makhno, whose voice rang out against oppression of all workers in the Ukraine, calling for us to rise up against the oppressors, marauders, and charlatans who tricked us. Our friend is at this moment on the march toward this final goal: freedom for all workers. "How do we think freedom

can be achieved? By the overthrow of all authority—monarchist, coalitions, republican, social democrat, Bolshevik-Communist—and, in its place, the creation of an independent soviet government, without authority or arbitrary legislative power. For the Soviet form of order is nothing like the authority of the social democratic. The Bolshevik-Communists call themselves a soviet government today. On the contrary, it is the highest form of an anti-authoritarian and anti-government soviet, and will express itself fully in the edification of a free community, living in harmony and independent of any authority, and in the social existence of the workers, in which each worker in particular and the community in general can autonomously build a happy and prosperous life based on the principles of solidarity, friendship, and equality for all.

"What is the conception of a soviet regime according to the Makhnovists? The workers must themselves choose their soviets, soviets

that accomplish the will and decisions of these same workers, in an executory, not an authoritarian fashion. The land, the factories, the mills, the mines, railroads, and other property of the people must belong to those who work in them; in other words they must be socialized.

"What means are the Makhnovists employing to reach this goal? The revolutionary, concerted, and intransigent struggle against all falsehood, arbitrariness, and oppression, whencesoever it may come. This is a struggle to the death, the struggle of a free world, a truthful goal, for which we bear arms. We call for the suppression of all governments, the destruction of the foundations of their lies, whether political, diplomatic, or economic. Only through the destruction of the state and social revolution will it be possible to achieve a true socialist soviet regime of the workers and peasants."

Alexander Skirda, *Nestor Makhno: Anarchist Cossack* (Paris: A.S., 1982). ∎

Had it not been for the Great War, Russia might have gone years, even decades, without a revolution against capitalism. With the war, it is objectively impossible: it's either the Revolution, or perish.

Lenin, 1917

east, the partisan chief, Nestor Makhno, an anarchist, held sway. Moreover, certain areas were occupied by German troops, and French detachments were camped along the Black Sea coast in the Crimea. Finally, there were local gangs of bandits, nearly everywhere.

In the fall of 1919, Denikin's troops occupied a large portion of the Ukraine and had forced the Red Army to retreat. In September, Kiev was taken by counterrevolutionary forces, first by Petlyura and then by Denikin, whose occupying forces carried out a brutal repression. In December, there was a third attempt to consolidate a Soviet regime in the Ukraine, with Denikin's defeat and the reoccupation of Karkov (December 12), Kiev (December 16), and Odessa (February 7, 1920). In February, Soviet authority was established in the main centers, but the unrest went on. A last attempt by the nationalists was launched by Petlyura, with military help from Poland and the political support of Joseph Pilsudski. After the Polish defeat, it would take yet another year to fully restore order, with sporadic fighting against Makhno's partisans continuing until August 1921 and against Petlyura's troops until the end of 1922.

The case of the Ukraine reveals the difficulties the Bolsheviks faced with the question of national identity. There had been two paths: incorporation pure and simple within the Soviet fold, or the creation of an independent Ukrainian Soviet authority, based on self-determination. By choosing the second course of action, the Soviets had run up against a serious obstacle: the absence of a local proletariat that was sufficiently strong and organized to ensure the spread of the communist ideology.

The Ukraine also offers a striking panorama of the multitude of forces that were in hot contention for control of the former empire. From 1918 to 1921, an exceptional level of chaos reigned in the whole region, with the most improbable alliances crystallizing overnight and disappearing just as quickly, between Bolsheviks, White Russians, Petlyurists, Makhnovists, and various other groups. The instability reigning in the former empire was such that by December 1919, Kiev had changed hands thirteen times and Ekaterinoslav nineteen times.

Karkov, 1920: Commissars arrive from Moscow to organize a communist government. Faced with the choice of direct incorporation of the Ukraine or creating an autonomous soviet entity, the Commissars chose the latter. The Ukrainian Socialist Republic entered the Union of Soviet Socialist Republics in 1922.
Ph © L'Illustration/Sygma

Chapter 4

WAR
AND **E**XPERIMENTATION

BESIEGED ON ALL SIDES, THE BOLSHEVIK REGIME WAS ABLE TO CONSOLIDATE ITS HOLD ON POWER THANKS TO TWO REMARKABLE TOOLS: THE RED ARMY, AGAINST FOREIGN AGGRESSORS, AND THE FEARED TCHEKA, AGAINST INTERNAL ENEMIES.

A t the outset of the civil war, few observers would have bet on the Soviet regime's chances of winning the day. The Allied powers that had chosen to intervene did so in the belief that the government in place was weak and would therefore be defeated in a few months. As for the Bolsheviks, they hoped that revolution would break out in Germany and that the international proletariat would support their cause, helping them secure the support of their own people in a culturally and economically underdeveloped Russia.

Within the Communist Party (which had replaced the Workers Social Democratic Party on March 8, 1918), the urban proletariat continued the crucial role it had played in the events of the Revolution. But in an essentially agricultural nation, the Soviet government was led to brutal acts of repression against those whom it had allowed to occupy the land, thus bringing into being, in a radical and definitive fashion, the long-awaited agrarian reform. It was only by force that the regime could obtain the supplies it needed to feed the cities and the army.

The civil war raged simultaneously along with numerous peasant revolts, the worst of which occurred in the summer of 1918 in the Volga region, and in March 1919 between the Volga and the Ural Mountains. In the cities, there were drastic food shortages, resulting in chaos and a rise in criminal activity. The hungry people often received bread mixed

The façade of Mary's Palace in Petrograd, decorated for the first of May in 1918. The situation in Russia was critical, with the first counterrevolutionary demonstrations and peasant revolts. The urban population was showing signs of growing discontent. The government worked against this lack of revolutionary enthusiasm by investing in two heavily centralized and disciplined entities: the Red Army and the Tcheka.
Ph © L'Illustration/Sygma

In the flux of a full-blown revolution, especially when it has been born of war, moderate, liberal, humanistic men will not be the ones to triumph. Democratic principles are for peace; in a Revolution, victory will belong to men of radical temperament.

Nikolai Berdyaev, 1937

with straw or other "substitutes"; in a daily fight for survival, people were forced to the black market. This was one of the principal traits of the civil war: the constant struggle for grain, a fight to the death for survival between city and country.

Violence and Terror

So how did communist Russia resist foreign invasion, economic isolation, famine, and epidemics? The ability to link the social question to nationalism, or rather nationalisms, was one of the determining factors in the success of the Soviet regime. The implementation of agrarian reform (the devolution of the land to the people) incited the peasants of Russia's vast territory to reject counterrevolutionary govern- ments that wanted to restore the old system by giving the land back to the great landlords. In addition, the White Russians did not encourage national claims: their program called not only for the restoration of feudalism, but also of White Russia's historic supremacy in the former empire. By their refusal to espouse local causes, they soon alienated the many partisans of national emancipation. Finally, a counterrevolution waged with foreign money and with the help of foreign armies made Russian peasants even more patriotic, and sometimes too, members of the intelligentsia. Thus, the Soviet regime's prestige came out considerably enhanced.

By the end of the civil war, when Russia was facing its historic enemy, Poland, the Bolsheviks were completely in character, as defenders of the Russian heritage and creators of a new national unity.

The second reason for the Bolsheviks' success was their capacity for organization and centralization, compared to their adversaries who were dispersed and divided among themselves. The White Russians were a group of highly competitive individuals whose insurmountable rivalries weakened their potential, often with disastrous effects. In contrast, the Bolsheviks armed themselves early on with the two most powerful pillars of any state: the Red Army to mobilize against foreign invaders, and the police (the Tcheka, or Extraordinary Commission against Counter-

revolution and Sabotage) to focus on enemies from within.

The civil war was a war of movement, marked by guerilla warfare and migrations of civilians. The Red Army's first days were chaotic and improvised, for it had constantly to absorb as many recruits as it could, as well as deal with columns of refugees and deserters. The organizational challenge was huge and the administrative structure mediocre and underequipped. But the conviction that "the people in arms" must have an army was a very powerful one, whose hold on people's minds never faltered.

After the Revolution, the Red Army of the Workers and Peasants was created (by decree of January 15, 1918) in the spirit of a popular, volunteer militia, democratically governed in the council tradition. The demands of the civil war would make it quite different in its final, fully-realized form. The transition from partisan army to an ordered, permanent structure was effected by resorting to the traditional method: conscription. Along with the draft came traditional military hierarchy, in which the talents and experience of former Czarist officers were put to use again. With

Funeral of the Chief of the Petrograd Tcheka, Moses Uritski, assassinated by a student affiliated with right-wing socialist revolutionaries. The central committee of this party had renounced violence after the fall of the Czar, but in 1918 the prevailing goal had become the overthrow of the Bolsheviks, with the help of the Allied Powers. On July 6, the German ambassador, von Mirbach, was assassinated, and, on August 30, a young woman, a militant socialist revolutionary, injured Lenin.
Ph © L'Illustration/Sygma

Arrest of a socialist revolutionary during the summer of 1918. The wave of assassinations provoked the hardening of the regime against all forms of opposition. On September 2, 1918, the Soviets announced that they would respond to "White Terror" with "Red Terror."
Ph © L'Illustration/Sygma

an ironclad discipline—the Communists were pitiless toward deserters—and a highly centralized organization, they achieved a state of total militarization of the economy and of society. The artisan of the Communist fighting machine was Leo Trotsky, who after a protracted negotiation with his colleagues in the Central Committee, obtained permission to hire former Czarist officers.

In addition to the class struggle, the Bolsheviks used what they called "Red Terror," even openly encouraging it in the countryside against rich landowners. Indeed, they believed it was completely acceptable and even necessary to use force and terror in a time of revolution. Only extraordinary measures would break the enemy's resistance, and were the only valid response to the intensifying of the counterrevolutionary threat, which was now materializing in political assassination, intrigue, and military action. In particular, certain socialist revolutionaries rekindled their faction's traditional spirit of violence.

In June of 1918, a highly popular Bolshevik leader, V.

Volodarski, was assassinated in Petrograd, and on July 6, Count Wilhelm von Mirbach, German Ambassador was. There was even a coup attempt in Moscow. During the summer, revolts and insurrections—some of which were organized by a well-known terrorist, Boris Savinkov, and others encouraged by the French—erupted in several cities (Yaroslavl, Murom, Nijni-Novgorod, and Rybinski). They were all brutally crushed.

At Ekaterinenburg in the Ural region, the local soviet, fearing the approach of the Czechoslovak legion, made the decision to execute Nicholas II and his family on July 18. On August 30, Lenin was injured by Fania Kaplan; on the same day, a student killed the chief of the Petrograd Tcheka, Moses Uritski. In early September—in a surprising analogy with a certain September during the French Revolution—the regime responded with a series of mass arrests and summary executions. The targets, in Petrograd as well as in Moscow, were members of the Socialist Revolutionary Party and representatives of the aristocracy, the financial sector, the Czarist Army, and generally anyone associated with bourgeois liberal professions.

The Red Terror was spearheaded by the Tcheka, which ruthlessly purged the proletarian dictatorship of its enemies. "The Extraordinary Commission," wrote Latsis,

Felix Dzerjinski (1877–1926), was a Polish revolutionary, a former collaborator of Rosa Luxemburg, and a member of the Revolutionary Committee of October. On December 7, 1917, he submitted the idea of a revolutionary police—the Tcheka—whose primary mission was to safeguard the regime against saboteurs within the administration, but also to repress crime and "anarchy" and put an end to pillage by bands of drunks.
Ph © Coll. Viollet

THE TCHEKIST

In the context of the Red Terror, Vladimir Zazubrin's remarkable novel, *The Tchekist*, is a representative case. Written in 1923 but censured for ideological reasons, it was finally published during the perestroika in 1989.

"In France, there was the guillotine and public executions. Here, we use the basement. Secret execution. In public, the death of a criminal, even the most dangerous one, receives a martyr's consecration, indeed, a hero's laurels. They give publicity to the enemy and boost its morale. The family receives a body to bury, says final words, accomplishes the last wishes of the defunct, knows the exact date of death. Destruction is not total. Secret execution, in a basement, without verdict or sentencing, stage or audience, this sudden death has a crushing effect on the enemy. It's an enormous, pitiless machine, that sucks in its victims like a magnet, and reduces them to pulp like a meat-grinder. After the execution, no one knows the date of their death, there is no body, no last words, no grave. Just emptiness. The enemy has been entirely destroyed."

Vladimir Zazubrin, *The Tchekist*, Bourgois, Paris 1990. ∎

"The Spider and the Flies," anti-clerical propaganda poster from October 1918. The text, by the proletarian Demian Bedny, describes the long labor of the Russian Pope, the "spider with the little cross" to capture the "peasant brothers": "The spider lives gaily, spinning its web, and catches flies, young and old, even Mujik fanatics. The flies buzz plaintively, bringing money to the spider, everything they earned with their sweat and blood."
Ph © BDIC

one of its chiefs, "is not an investigative body nor a court of law. It is a combat weapon, operating on the interior front, and using the resources of prosecution, tribunals, and the Army. The Tcheka does not judge the enemy; it strikes them down."

Indeed, the Tcheka's power was virtually limitless. In a country paralyzed by chaos, crisscrossed by lethal lines of tension, the Commission exercised its own form of dictatorship, administering "justice" with the most extreme rigor. Dozens of "counter-revolutionary organizations" were discovered, accused of being financed by foreign governments and composed of officers of the former regime or other constitutional or democratic elements, and their members annihilated. In reality, little effort was made to determine the true nature of these groups.

The Tcheka also judged cases of corruption and speculation, punishing embezzlement and various other crimes. Generally, cases were cursorily investigated and trials were totally secret, with no defense witnesses allowed; verdicts were handed down without hearing the accused. Abuses were rampant. According to official Tcheka archives, 12,733 people were executed in Russia between 1918 and 1920. These figures account for only a part of the total, for they do not include the activities of the Tcheka's many local branches all over Russia. Historians estimate the actual toll of the Extraordinary Commission between 1917 and 1922 to be as high as 140,000 victims.

However, one must place this in the perspective of the total number of victims of the savage reprisals, massacres, and other atrocities of the civil war. The perpetrators were on all sides: Skoropadski's reactionary government in the Ukraine and its armed forces supported by the Germans (May–November 1918); brigands pillaging in the countryside; and peasants revolting against the landowners. Denikin's troops massacred civilians in the northern Caucasus and in Daghestan in the spring and summer of 1919; Petlyura set off pogroms against the Ukrainian Jews in July 1919. Some of the worst atrocities were committed by Kolchak's troops as their leader had failed to win over the people—a precondition for staying in power without foreign support. In the autumn of 1919, there was an epidemic of desertions, with over 20,000 of Kolchak's men—an entire regiment—disappearing with their weapons and supplies.

Globally, the dictatorship exercised by both sides, Bolsheviks and counterrevolutionaries, to keep or gain control of the vast Russian territory, the savagery of police and military repression (especially that of the Tcheka) in the entire country, the massacres both Red and White, were to leave a profound imprint on people's minds, and would also stamp the Revolution's future with the seal of violence.

On January 19, 1918, Tikhon, Patriarch of Moscow, in an appeal to the clergy and all believers, declared anathema on the communists. In response, the Soviet government published a decree on "the freedom of worship and religious societies" (January 20) and proclaimed the separation of church and state, and of church and school (23 January). Sentenced to house arrest in 1922, Tikhon was freed two years later after agreeing to a declaration of loyalty to the Soviet government.
Ph © L'Illustration/Sygma

A New Society

A few weeks after the Revolution, Maxim Gorky denounced the success of the Bolsheviks. On December 10, 1917 he wrote in his newspaper *The New Life*: "The Commissars of the People are using Russia as a proving ground; the Russian people are being treated like a horse injected with typhus in order to recover a serum from its blood. Like mad scientists, the Commissars are carrying out a cruel and inhuman experiment on the Russian people, without realizing that, starved and completely exhausted, this poor horse just might drop dead."

These words might have been even more prophetic

than their author intended them to be, considering the lack of preparation the Bolsheviks had in building a new society. Some years later, Lenin's wife, Nadezhda Krupskaya, remembered that when names were being proposed for the Commissar positions, some of those designated tried to refuse, alleging their incompetence. Lenin, apparently, replied sarcastically, "Do you think any of us is competent?" Indeed, no one had experience in government, and so the leaders emphasized that a Commissar had to be a new kind of Minister: one that organized and led different sectors of the administration's activities, while being in direct contact with the masses.

An internationally known personality, Maxim Gorky, the social democrat writer (1868–1938), considered the Revolution to be a fatal mistake. He expounded his argument in his newspaper, The New Life, *which was banned by Bolshevik censorship on July 16, 1918. Later, Gorky the "heretic" would become the guru of socialist realism under Stalin.*
Ph © L'Illustration/Sygma

With the Bolsheviks in power, socialism became an essentially economic issue—the Bolsheviks' Achilles heel. The importance of an economic plan had been under-estimated, even forgotten. In early October 1917, however, Yuri Larin, an ex-Menshevik who was to become one of the foremost theorists of the communist economy, complained publicly that the Bolsheviks' economic ideas were "almost meaningless." The Bolsheviks did have a plan of sorts: they envisaged nationalization of credit institutions, fused into one state bank and of the great oil, steel, and coal monopolies, then in the hands of shareholders, as well as the creation of a cartel of medium-sized businesses. Moreover, the people were to organize themselves into consumer cooperatives, with oversight on production and distribution.

In the spring of 1917, the Bolsheviks had repeatedly stressed that modern capitalism had its own process of progressive "socialization" of some sectors of the economy and that the foundations for a non-commercial economy had already been laid. In Russia, this tendency toward state control of trade and the distribution of goods could be reinforced by an impetus from below, from the grassroots of society. This led to an innovative response to problems of penury and logistics resulting from the crisis, with workers taking matters into their own hands. Faced with runaway inflation and shortages, they intervened directly in the market by resorting to exchanges in kind, trading in the most basic fashion to ensure their subsistence. Increasingly, peasants would refuse cash payment. "What is paper good for?" they would say.

Well before the October Revolution, the Bolshevik leaders, already faced with the disruption of the entire Russian economy, formally proposed the institution of a system of direct trade, controlled by worker and Soviet deputies, in the following products: tools, clothing, and shoes, against wheat and other foodstuffs. Lenin's writings refer on two occasions in 1917 to this form of circulation of goods: in an agrarian reform bill presented to the first peasants' pan-Russian Congress and in a bill on the struggle against economic ruin, put forth in the first congress of factory committees in Petrograd.

At the very beginning of the Revolution, a volunteer militia of the people received the mission to defend the Soviet republic. It would soon become the Red Army.
Ph © L'Illustration/Sygma

The theoretical positions of Lenin were in general in line with those of other Marxists of his time. Socialism is presented as the opposite of capitalism, and if capitalism's defining features are the market and money, socialism's is to eliminate the merchant and monetary economy. On December 4, 1917, before the representatives of the workers' Soviet of Petrograd, Lenin declared, "Economic necessity led Russia to resort to trade in kind, the very essence of the socialist economy."

In his view, the socialist economy needed to be organized into communal networks of producers and

Leo Davidovitch Trotsky (1879–1940) was born in Yanovka, in Kerson province of the Ukraine. An early militant revolutionary, he was arrested in 1897 and sentenced two years later to four years of exile in eastern Siberia for his activities with workers' associations in southern Russia. He escaped in 1902 and emigrated to London, where he met Lenin, Plekhanov, and Martov and wrote for the communist newspaper, *Iskra*. During the Congress of Brussels in 1903 that marked the schism of Bolsheviks and Mensheviks, Trotsky sided with the Mensheviks, and declared himself opposed to the Leninist conception of a centralized party. In 1905, he returned to Russia and became president of the Petrograd Soviet during the Revolution. Imprisoned afterward, he worked on his theory of permanent revolution. Sent to Siberia, he escaped again, reaching London in 1907, then Vienna, where he remained until 1914. After a brief sojourn in Zurich and Paris, he emigrated to the United States. Back in Russia for the February Revolution, he approached the Bolsheviks and received the Petrograd Soviet again, his headquarters as leader of the Petrograd revolution in October. As Commissar of the People for Foreign Affairs he concluded the Treaty of Brest-Litovsk with Germany (1918). Then, as Commissar of War, he became the father of the great Red Army. At Lenin's death in 1924, he opposed the rise of Stalin; in 1927, he was expelled from the Party; in 1929, he was banished from the USSR for life; and, in 1931, he was stripped of his Soviet citizenship. He died in Mexico nine years later at the hand of one of Stalin's secret police.

"The permanent revolution, as Marx defined it, is a kind of revolution that cannot negotiate with any form of class domination. It does not stop at the democratic stage, but implements socialist measures and declares war

on reaction abroad. The seed of each phase of this revolution is contained in the preceding one, and it will only stop with the liquidation of all class distinctions. The theory of permanent revolution, which reappeared in 1905, showed that, in our time, a backwardly bourgeois country, in order to achieve democracy, is directly led to the dictatorship of the proletariat, and that this dictatorship takes socialist forms of action. That is the fundamental tenet of this theory. While in the traditional view the path to the dictatorship of the proletariat is long, and necessitates a lengthy democratic transition, the theory of permanent revolution held that in a backward country, the path to democracy was the dictatorship of the proletariat. In consequence, democracy was not considered an end in itself, valid decades into the future, but an immediate prelude to the socialist revolution to which it is linked indissolubly. Thus the revolutionary process from democratic revolution to social transformation in society became a permanent one."

Leon Trotsky, *The Permanent Revolution*, Berlin, 1930 (Russian edition). ∎

Leon Trotsky, surrounded by his staff, reviews troops in Moscow. Tireless organizer of the Red Army, Trotsky was able to allow ex-Czarist officers and ex-revolutionary leaders into its ranks, after a difficult battle with left-wing socialist revolutionaries and communists, who promoted the idea of a partisan army and opposed bringing in former members of the Imperial Army.
Ph © L'Illustration/Sygma

consumers exchanging goods without recourse to currency. Distribution would be on an egalitarian basis. The key element of the system was the obligatory organization of the Russian population into consumer cooperatives given the role of managing the distribution of goods —the "cells of socialist society"—and the state monopoly on the trade in wheat and other staple foods. On January 8, 1918 in Petrograd, before 60 of the principal militants of his party, Lenin stated that "the reorganization of Russia according to the dictatorship of the proletariat, with nationalization of banks and big industries, and the exchange of consumer goods and food between the cities and the

Soldiers of the Red Army in training. The intervention of the Allies, the rise of peasant opposition, and general chaos pushed Soviet Russia along the path of rigorously centralized authority. But this was also to entail the progressive extension of authoritarian methods in the general organization of society and the economy.
Ph © L'Illustration/Sygma

peasant consumer cooperatives is perfectly feasible, on the condition that we can dispose of a few months of peaceful labor. This reorganization will render socialism indestructible in Russia and invincible in the world."

These theoretical foundations were to confront the grim reality of daily life in Russia. The European war had left Russia in a state of total chaos. The interior crisis was the top priority for the revolution, with three main areas to address: hunger, unemployment, and anarchy. The Treaty of Brest-Litovsk had dispossessed

Russia of a third of its population and its agricultural land, roughly four-fifths of its coalmines, and half of its heavy industry. The conversion from a wartime economy to a peacetime economy was then brutally interrupted by the civil war and foreign intervention. The various fronts cut off industries from their supply of raw materials, and many factories were forced to close down. According to data from the industrial census of 1918, on August 31, out of 9,750 factories, 3,690, or 38 percent, were inactive. In 1920, industrial production was barely 15 percent of the pre-war level, and in the Ukraine, it was 10 percent. Transportation was hardest hit, and in 1920, agricultural output was

Coat of arms of imperial Russia
Ph © L'Illustration/Sygma

THE ROMANOV DYNASTY (1613–1917)

Mikhail Romanov (1613–1645)

Alexis, the Very Peaceful (1645–1676)

Sophia, Regent (1682–1689)	**Fyodor III** (1676–1682)	**Ivan V**, Co-Regent (1682–1689)	**Peter the Great** (1682–1725) (from his second wife Martha Skavronska)

Caterina	**Anne** (1730–1740)		**Catherine I** (1725–1727)

Elizabeth (Anna Leopoldovna), Regent (1740–1741)	Alexis (from the first marriage)	Anna	**Elizabeth** (1741–1762)

Ivan VI (1740–1741)	**Peter II** (1727–1730)	**Peter III** (1762) (married Sophia d'Anhalt-Zerbst) **Caterina the Great** (1762–1796)	

Pavel I (1796–1801)

Alexander I (1801–1825)	**Nikolai I** (1825–1855)

Alexander II (1855–1881)

Alexander III (1881–1894)

Nikolai II (1894–1917)

After the uprisings of July 1917, the Kerenski government decided to transfer the Romanov family from their residence in Czarskoie Selo to Tobolsk, in Siberia. Here, the Great-Duchess Tatiana carries sod, with the help of a soldier.

Ph © L'Illustration/Sygma

still only a little more than half that of 1913, with the portion brought into the market representing a quarter of previous levels (20–25 percent less cultivated land in Russia, 20 percent less in the Ukraine, and 30 percent less in Belarus).

Development According to Lenin

Until the beginning of the civil war, the passage from a bourgeois economy to a socialist one was envisioned with prudence. The revolution did not seem ready to lay the foundations of a new economy. It had simply defeated the economic power of the landowners and the political authority of the bourgeoisie. So-called "scientific socialism," absorbed in its critique of the capitalist order, never really elaborated a theory of socialist order. In 1918 and 1919, it was time to move from the negative phase of the destruction of capitalism to the positive phase of building a communist society. Were the Bolsheviks ready for the task?

A communist society could not limit itself to the expropriation of factories, of the landowners, and all the means of production; it could not simply control production and distribute products. It had also to implement the following principle: "From each according to his capacities, to each according to his needs." From the beginning, the Bolsheviks had touted egalitarianism. But this was more of an ideologically dictated line of conduct than a rigorous economic system. It proceeded from a vision of leveling differences and eliminating the class society. Certainly the land decree had incorporated the key concept of peasant justice into socialist law, distributing the land to those who worked it. The decree on worker control facilitated takeovers of factories. However, while in the countryside a new tendency to small landownership was emerging, in the cities, industrial installations, after a few initial hesitations, were quickly nationalized and centralized. In the area of commerce and distribution, the Bolsheviks simply reestablished the

The Czar and his family, in Tobolsk, sunbathing on the roof of a greenhouse. After the October Revolution, the regional soviet of the Ural was granted a request to have the prisoners brought to Ekaterinenburg. In July 1918, they were be executed there and their remains destroyed.
Ph © L'Illustration/Sygma

Nikolai Bukarin (1888–1938), leader of the left-wing communists, considered the Treaty of Brest-Litovsk a betrayal of the European proletariat. He spoke out against compromising with private capitalism and demanded the total nationalization of the means of production.
Ph © Coll. Viollet

monopoly of the Kerenski government on wheat; in the finance sector, the nationalization of banks was approved.

In the first days of the Revolution, the Bolsheviks emphasized the moderate points of their program. In response to the left-wing communists, in particular Nicholas Bukarin, for whom full-fledged communism was just around the corner, Lenin's line was that the path to communism was to be long, that the terrain still had to be prepared, that it was too soon to speak of abolishing the state, and that gradual measures were in order.

In many cases, this meant simply giving a communist legislative form to measures of self-protection that workers had already obtained long ago under the bourgeois regime (for example, the eight-hour workday). Sometimes, it meant implementing agrarian reforms that were massively demanded by the peasants and that all the progressive political forces were loudly rooting for (to wit, the confiscation of the land from the great landowners and its devolution to the peasants without payment). In still other cases it meant validating and radicalizing certain new tendencies that had emerged from the evolution of international capitalism—for example, state control over the production and distribution of goods.

Of course, more extremist statements and dogmatic declarations couched in ideology were not absent from revolutionary discourse. But, for a time, they coexisted with more pervasive assertions emphasizing "reform" and "evolution." Russia had not yet attained the final phase of development, and the Bolsheviks were ready to accept the consequences of belatedness. Appeals were sent out to "national entrepreneurs" and "bourgeois specialists" to collaborate in building socialism, a delicate process. Indeed, capitalism had taken hold only recently in Russia, and this resulted in the coexistence of societies and developmental tendencies that were very different, sometimes even violently opposed.

The model that was adopted in the spring of 1918 was that of "state capitalism" practiced by Germany during the war. Lenin repeatedly stressed that only when production was sufficiently socialized and in the most mature stage of capitalist development could the success of a socialist model of production be

THE DEGENERACY OF THE SOVIETS

The Russian word "soviet," meaning "council," was to achieve worldwide renown, thanks to the specific political meaning conferred on it by the October Revolution, and already to a certain extent by the events of 1905. The Bolshevik victory radically transformed the word's meaning: the original councils of democratic management—really the engines of the first days of revolution—were reduced to being the gearbox or transmission that enabled the party to drive the masses.

In 1917, the soviets had become the Bolsheviks' primary instrument in the conquest of power ("All power to the soviets!"). Afterward, their only use was to serve as symbols of Bolshevik domination. With the October Revolution, the Bolsheviks created a state that was to embody the dictatorship of the proletariat, with the soviets playing the role of the executive; "soviet" authority was thus presented as a new form of democracy, founded upon the autonomous participation of dozens of millions of workers in the running of the state.

Representing workers, peasants, soldiers, and politicians, the soviets were to organize the masses under the leadership of one party, eliminating the distinction between those who governed and those who were governed. After October, the other socialist parties were outlawed, preventing the formation of a non-Bolshevik majority within the soviets. In the summer of 1918, the Bolshevik Party had a monopoly on political existence in Russia; democracy in the councils had received a death sentence, for these were henceforth no more than the instruments of the domination of a disciplined minority of professional revolutionaries over the masses. Rosa Luxemburg, the German revolutionary, gave perhaps the most detailed description of the degeneracy of the soviets, in 1918, only a few months after the Bolsheviks' triumph:

"Lenin and Trotsky made the soviets into the only representative body of the working masses, instead of the ones resulting from general elections. But if

political life in the country is suffocated, the soviets are too. Without general elections, without freedom of the press or freedom to assemble, without unfettered competition of ideas, life will inexorably depart from all public institutions; the only one that will not become a vegetable will be the bureaucracy. Public opinion will drift off to sleep; the only ones awake will be a few dozen leaders, who by their inexhaustible energy and idealism will govern the affairs of the land. Real power lies with a dozen super-intelligent men, and the elite of the workers is sometimes invited to hear one of their brilliant speeches and vote unanimously in favor of whatever is proposed. In other words, government by a clique; not the dictatorship of the proletariat, but that of a few politicians. A bourgeois dictatorship, Jacobinite, hegemonic."

Rosa Luxemburg, *The Russian Revolution*, Socialist Party Ed., 1922. ∎

*R*ussia embarked on the path of proletarian revolution, not because its economy was ready for socialist transformation, but because the economy could no longer continue to develop on the basis of capitalism.

Leon Trotsky, 1935

guaranteed. Indeed, it was the First World War that accelerated the concentration of businesses and of capital. It introduced governments to national planning and state control over production. It forced governments to calculate precisely the needs of the population in urban and rural areas, mobilize human and material resources, and redistribute investment, raw materials, and foodstuffs. In brief, the war set off the transition from private to state capitalism. "The proletariat," said Lenin, "takes the weapons of capitalism, and does not invent them from scratch."

Europe too had experienced this expansion of the state's role in the economy. In Soviet Russia, an attempt would be made to prolong this development to its natural limit. The monopoly on wheat, rationing cards, obligatory employment, and the like are not the inventions of the egalitarian ideology or the collectivist mentality of the Bolsheviks. These measures had already been taken in the most advanced European countries involved in the war effort.

In the Bolsheviks' view, these measures were to be a powerful means to organize the economy of the proletarian state, which entailed taking an inventory of the national wealth and achieving effective control over production and distribution. With the participation of the workers, the state implemented efforts never before witnessed to overcome capitalists' resistance and subjugate them to the will of the proletariat. "These means of control and the obligation to work," said Lenin, "will be more powerful than the laws and the guillotine of the French Revolution." Methods of socialist management were borrowed from German practices during the war. According to the Bolshevik leader, history had taken such a strange turn that, by 1918, it had engendered "two separate halves of socialism," side by side, exactly like "two future chicks in the incubator of international imperialism." Germany and Russia respectively embodied the fulfilled economic conditions and political conditions for socialism.

For the moment, the "German Revolution" had not taken place. The Soviet regime's task was nevertheless to implement the German model of state

capitalism and assimilate it entirely, using authoritarian methods if necessary. Lenin's comment on this was that Peter the Great had done the same thing, when he used barbaric means to vanquish barbarism in Russia.

The October Revolution had a huge impact on women's lives. After the decree on divorce, civil marriage, and civil status in December 1917, the first Family Code, promulgated September 18, 1918, established the equality of political and civil rights for men and women. Here, in Petrograd in 1918, a woman votes for the first time.
Ph © Coll. Viollet

Chapter 5

WAR **C**OMMUNISM

BEING IN A STATE OF WAR ENABLED RUSSIA TO STAGE A LIVING EXPERIMENT IN COMMUNISM WITH THE INTRODUCTION OF A "NATURAL" ECONOMY. BUT WOULD A SYSTEM THAT HAD PROVEN USEFUL IN WAR SURVIVE IN A TIME OF PEACE?

T he hesitations and uncertainty that were characteristic of the first phase of socialist management disappeared with the start of the civil war. In the fall of 1918, the economic crisis and the paralysis of distribution triggered the implementation of a socio-economic system that was later to be dubbed "war communism."

War communism designated a series of temporary and extraordinary measures that the Soviets put into place from late 1918 to early 1921 in the context of the counterrevolution and foreign intervention. The Bolsheviks did more than just pass emergency measures like any power involved in a war effort. They also modified the patterns of economic and social policy, and they ended up inverting the two main axes of their program: on the one hand, they abandoned the idea of a slow transition to communism, with a worker-controlled state; and on the other, they embraced more and more overtly the idea of an immediate passage to collectivist forms of organization.

The unique character of the system that would emerge in Russia after the October Revolution lies in the integration of emergency policies adopted during the war within a coherent "peacetime" socialist system.

In the heart of Russia, in the great marketplace of Samara, representatives from villages paralyzed by shortages arrive with huge horse- and camel-drawn wagons, in search of seed for the next harvest. The revolutionary period was marked by constant famine, in the beginning limited mostly to the cities and the army, due to disrupted distribution networks and the decrease of cultivated land. Then, in 1920, came a terrible drought.
Ph © L'Illustration/Sygma

We don't claim that Marx or that Marxists know all the concrete aspects of the path to socialism. That would be absurd. We know the direction of the path, we know the class patterns that lead to it; but what it is concretely, will be shown by the experience of millions of men.

Lenin, 1917

Communism and Distribution

The project of a total and immediate socialist system encountered the obstacle of the countryside. The Land Decree gave the land to the peasants, cancelled leases and debts to former landowners, and spurred rural Russia to organize itself on the basis of agrarian reform. But there was never a direct and lasting relationship between the struggle of the peasants and that of their urban counterparts. On the contrary, two different conceptions of the economy and of society would chronically oppose each other.

The reforms satisfied the ambitions of the peasants as a class—to own individually the land they worked on. On their side, the workers, occupiers, and self-appointed managers of factories sought to realize a truly collectivist form of production. Between the Land Decree and the decree on worker control, it seemed possible to believe in the political unification of the proletariat. But private material interests would quickly revive old divisions. As soon as industry became incapable of satisfying demand in the rural areas, the exchange of products with the cities was blocked with class confrontation the inevitable result.

Newly made landowners, the peasants saw in agrarian reform an opportunity to establish trade in a free market. Well before the October Revolution, however, the temporary government had established that it had the sole right to buy and sell wheat. On March 25, 1917, faced with the distribution crisis, this was extended to all grain products; after the October Revolution the Soviet government would reassert the state's monopoly. In this way, the peasants' first harvest was already subject to a system that was the opposite of a free market. Moreover, they were immediately obligated to deliver their surplus to the state at a fixed price. Even this was insufficient to ensure adequate distribution of wheat to the non-peasant population, and, consequently, one of the most controversial measures of war communism was introduced: the forced requisition of wheat from the peasants (*prodrazvertska*). Two decrees in May of 1918 formally gave the Commissariat full power to implement this measure. During the second half of 1918, forced requisitions were carried out in the Tula, Viatsk, Kaluga, and Volga provinces. The decree of January 11, 1919 extended the requisitions to all Soviet territory, followed by the Ukraine, Turkestan, and Siberia in 1920.

Requisitioning enabled the government to seize surplus grain and hay—and sometimes more than the surplus—to supply the army and the urban population. Soon potatoes and beef were included. By the end of 1920, requisitioning had extended to almost all agricultural products. Harvests were overseen by armed detachments (*prodotriady*) composed of workers, soldiers, and sailors recruited as volunteers and sent into the countryside. They used the Poor Peasants' Committees as relays, and worked in close collaboration with the local soviets. The first detachments formed spontaneously in November 1917, and were then integrated into the Commissariat for distribution by the decree of May 27, 1918. In November 1918 the prodotriady numbered 72,000 men, and in 1919–1920, from 55,000 to 82,000.

The Revolution enabled peasants to take possession of the land: 20 million farmers tilled miniscule lots of land with the most primitive equipment. As soon as the state attempted to control agriculture and implement requisitions, the peasants lost all interest in production, rejected the market, and reverted to subsistence farming.
Ph © L'Illustration/Sygma

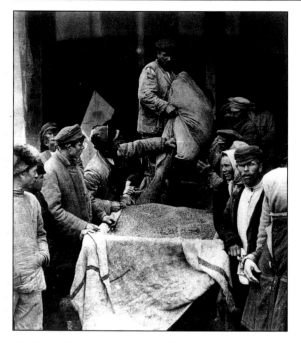

Distribution of wheat to the peasants at Samara. In early 1919, attempts were made to organize collective farms (the first Kholkoz) in order to work the land more rationally and increase productivity.

Ph © L'Illustration/Sygma

The interdiction of the wheat trade resulted in the creation of a flourishing black market. In the meantime, the primary means of exchange—money—had completely disappeared, so it became necessary to return to barter. The collapsing economy, hunger in the cities and industrial centers, and land redistribution spurred millions of people to migrate to the countryside. Multitudes of workers deserted factories and drifted into rural areas, seeking food. Some found work in the fields, and some as artisans or even as speculators. The peasants' spirit of initiative rose to the occasion: the countryside, in spite of decreased agricultural production, still boasted reserves. But these were exchanged only against necessary products, such as matches, salt, shoes, and oil. City dwellers had to take with them to the country every imaginable piece of merchandise to trade against a few kilos of potatoes or flour.

It was the time of the *meshochniki* (bag people), men and women who took the train to faraway villages with a bag (*meshok*) on their shoulders, looking for bread and other foodstuffs. In early 1920, a pound of soap was worth a pound of lard; three yards of linen cloth garnered 100 kilos of hemp, and three pounds of starch, 100 pounds of potatoes. The market was officially abolished, but almost every town or city had a place where barter was openly practiced. The market in Moscow, next to the Sukarev Tower built by Peter the Great in 1692, was traditionally a place where merchandise of all types was exchanged, from foodstuffs to used books. From time to time the police would carry out an inspection, but usually it left the place alone. The black market of Moscow became so popular that the word *sukarevka* passed into the local slang as a synonym of private "free" trade and speculation.

The illegal transport of goods in the whole country (*meshochnichestvo*) attained immense proportions. In May 1918, according to the Commissariat of Supply records, in the Kursk province alone, up to 40,000 puds (a pud equals 35 pounds) of wheat were transported in 24 hours. The government employed every means to combat this phenomenon, organizing brigades of inspectors and police roadblocks, and rigorously enforcing limits on the transport of products from the countryside to the cities—all in vain, for during the war almost half of all produce transported in the country was carried by these "bag people."

War communism turned out to be a long series of extraordinary decrees that would concentrate all the material and human resources of the country in the hands of the central authorities. In the interests of the country's defense and the people's protection, the state became the sole decision-maker concerning the destination and the utilization of goods and people. All industry was run by the state. Nationalization was intensified from the summer of 1919 onward, and it extended to small and medium-sized businesses the decree of June 28, 1918 that had been limited to large industry. A strictly centralized economy was put into place, through a system called *glavkizm* (based on committees or

Young members of the Extraordinary Commission for the Struggle against Counterrevolution and Sabotage (the Tcheka). Fighting illegal trade was one of the Tcheka's missions, but in spite of severe repression against speculation, the black market still accounted for two-thirds of all merchandise entering the cities.
Ph © L'Illustration/Sygma

Money will lose its meaning. Money only has value when production is not organized; the more it is organized, the weaker the role played by money. In consequence, the need for money will eventually disappear.

Bukarin, 1918

glavki, directing the various sectors of industry). The people were brought under the obligation to enroll in consumer cooperatives.

Products of mass consumption were distributed according to strict norms; wages were almost always paid in kind. The people received basic goods (bread, sugar, salt, matches, soap, and kerosene) with coupons good for an individual ration. A monthly salary could be made up of 25 pounds of bread, eight pounds of meat or fish, a half a pound of lard, eighteen pounds of vegetables, a pound of coffee, and two boxes of matches. At first, rations were distributed independently of the number of hours worked. The only rule was "No work, no food." In a letter to workers in Petrograd, Lenin called this rule the "central, fundamental, essential tenet of socialism," an axiom that "is understandable by every worker" and must be defended "by all workers, all poor peasants, and even better-off peasants; all those who have known need, all those who have lived by their work." Later, other criteria were introduced, which took into account social class and the amount of work accomplished by each individual.

Even paid services would be progressively abolished. Water, electricity, heat, the postal, telegraph, and telephone services, public baths, transportation, housing—all of these were directly supplied by the state free of charge. In exchange, citizens were bound by a kind of "social contract": the adult population was constantly mobilized under the obligatory work program, according to Article 18 of the July 1918 Constitution and the Labor Code (December 1918). From early 1919 onward, recruitment into the Red Army and the dispersion of workers into the countryside took their toll on the work force; this led to a veritable militarization of labor in the form of worker brigades, which were run with an iron discipline. Henceforth, strikes were considered a form of treason, the industrial equivalent of mutinies in the military.

Down with Money!

The belated abolition of serfdom in Russia meant that the traditional barter economy continued to subsist in certain areas. At the turn of the century, the Russian people were mainly preoccupied with satisfying their immediate needs. Their wariness toward money was brilliantly expressed by Joseph Suprup, a factory worker, in a letter addressed to Lenin in January 1919: "If you consider life with common sense, who needs this cursed money? Life means food, clothing, a roof over one's head, and then the rest! As for me, the son of a poor peasant, I can see clearly that the worker and the peasant can live very happily without this bourgeois metal and paper detritus that is money. If we get rid of money, it will also end the lazy existence of the bourgeoisie and speculators. 'He who doesn't work, doesn't eat.' Soviet Russia, as the first socialist republic, should make a point of initiating the destruction of the calamity that is money, replacing it with formalized compensation in kind for each person's work. I think that is feasible."

Market in the countryside. During the civil war, Moscow and Petrograd each lost several hundred thousand inhabitants. The economic debacle was so severe that no big city was immune from the exodus to rural areas, where food was more readily available.
Ph © L'Illustration/Sygma

*S*ketch for a mural entitled "The Foundry," by M. I. Agulianski, for the first anniversary celebration of the October Revolution on November 7, 1918 in Petrograd Ph © Coll. part./D.R.

The attempt to abolish money is a very special phenomenon within war communism. The first revolutionary writings had envisioned the possibility, although with reservations. In the communist program, Nikolai Bukarin wrote, "our society is evolving into a vast society of workers, who produce and distribute without recourse to money." The leader of the left-wing communists was convinced that the era of money was nearing its end.

According to a decree promulgated January 23, 1919, accounts between businesses and administrative bodies were to be concluded without monetary transactions or compensations. Economic relationships were to play out on balance sheets, with records of sums owed or received. Now, paper money served only for modest transactions. Indeed, the fact that most essential goods and services were free rendered money useless. The regime's goal was indeed to eliminate money entirely, in accordance with the idea that transferring production in its entirety to the state would modify the terms of all economic exchange; that socialization of production would lead to the socialization of trade. Given that all the factories and everything they produced belonged to the state, money could be replaced by a strict accounting of the passage of goods from one commissariat to another and their distribution to the various state-controlled organizations. And, since the State decided what each product was worth and how much of it each citizen was entitled to, money would lose its function as a measure of value.

The Bolshevik Party program presented at the Eighth Congress in March 1919 stated that "in the initial phase of the transition from capitalism to communism... it is impossible to eliminate money." However, governmental action toward this end was envisioned in Article 15: "Based on bank nationalizations, the Russian Communist Party will endeavor to adopt policies aiming to enlarge the sphere of non-monetary compensation and to lay the groundwork for the elimination of money; i.e., the

Payment in kind was at its height at the end of the civil war, when 94 percent of wages were paid in essential goods and only six percent paid in currency. The inception of the New Economic Policy would progressively restore the use of money in the social and economic life of the country.

WORKERS' WAGES

The barter economy during the years 1917–1920 and its phasing out after 1921 were studied by Stanislas Strumilin, an economist, Director of the Commission for General State Planning (gosplan), in an analysis of the relationship between payment in kind and productivity in Russian industry. The following table gives an estimate of the average wages of Russian workers, calculated in rubles, from 1917–1922.

	wages in Moscow		wages in Petrograd		wages in Russia	
	monetary	in kind	monetary	in kind	monetary	in kind
1917						
I semester	23.20	—	34.70	0.46	19.30	0.23
II semester	16.30	0.48	17.50	1.80	13.80	1.14
1918						
I semester	5.40	1.02	4.55	1.73	5.42	1.38
II semester	3.41	1.56	2.79	1.56	4.04	1.56
1919						
I semester	1.44	2.31	1.62	2.73	1.82	2.56
II semester	1.06	1.79	1.01	3.15	0.99	2.27
1920						
I trimester	0.46	2.70	0.51	2.88	0.57	2.60
II trimester	0.43	2.21	0.48	2.46	0.42	2.41
III trimester	0.59	2.01	0.48	2.72	0.46	2.01
IV trimester	0.57	3.40	0.50	2.29	0.51	3.47
1921						
I trimester	0.24	4.34	0.26	3.33	0.23	3.13
II trimester	0.24	3.48	0.28	3.18	0.16	2.13
III trimester	1.40	3.20	1.00	2.92	0.61	1.82
IV trimester	6.26	3.51	3.38	3.26	2.85	4.33
1922						
I trimester	4.51	4.55	3.50	4.23	2.02	4.15
II trimester	7.28	3.63	5.68	3.07	3.23	3.84
III trimester	11.54	2.59	11.16	2.78	6.10	2.68
IV trimester	16.03	0.96	14.95	2.39	7.14	2.31

Russians wait in line in front of a store. Seven-tenths of workers' wages were spent on food. To survive, workers had to find supplementary sources of income; these usually took the form of illicit activities such as factory theft.
Ph © Keystone

obligation to deposit all money at the National Bank and the generalization of savings accounts, checkbooks, and of short-term coupons for various goods."

Speeches warning of the dangers of an abrupt transition to a "natural" economy soon became more rare. State ownership, which progressed with the course of the civil war, along with the elimination of the market, seemed to embody true socialism. Toward the middle of 1920, nearly everyone thought it was time for an economic system where money played no part.

Inflation and devaluation would also prove powerful catalyzers. Reduced industrial and agricultural output, diminished productivity, and the high cost of living made inflation rampant to such an extent that some economists envisioned harnessing the inflationary process to render the ruble utterly valueless, "resetting" the odometer, so to speak, by printing huge quantities of paper money. By flooding the country with rubles, the currency would eventually lose all value, hastening its total elimination. "Long live the printing press!" wrote Yevgeni Preobrayenski. "It doesn't have much time left, but it has already done three-fourths of its duty. In the archives of the great proletarian revolution, there will be cannons, rifles, and machine guns, and there will also be the printing press. The People's Commissariat of Finance has its own machine gun, and has shot the bourgeois order full of holes, using its own weapon against it. The laws of monetary circulation have become the very means to destroy the old regime and to finance the revolution."

War communism has long been considered by communist militants to be the first step in the transition to socialism. But in fact, the system was flawed by its artificial and arbitrary character. The result of an exceptional conjunction of circumstances, it lacked a sufficiently solid social and economic basis to last, once the state of emergency had ended. War communism was an attempt to manage the country's dwindling resources, to share and consume them rationally. Its most important consequences were the decline of industrial production, the end of the state's role as distributor of taxed consumer goods, the rapid

Bread for sale at the Moscow market on Sukharev Square. Clandestine markets attracted huge crowds every day in every city in Russia. State ownership and control of production and consumption strongly contributed to the development of a parallel economy.
Ph © L'Illustration/Sygma

spread of clandestine private commerce with constantly rising prices, and the unstoppable devaluation of the ruble. Some of its features, though, would prove durable: a highly complex and strictly centralized administrative apparatus announced the bureaucratic vocation of socialism.

The result was an obvious discrepancy between an envisioned "production communism" that had no chance of success in a system of state-owned industry and the reality of "distribution communism," which took advantage of traditional military structures that ensured delivery of goods through the use of force. This lack of coherence was compounded by the contradiction between deficient organization and

BOLSHEVIK PSYCHOLOGY THROUGH

Known by his pseudonym, Martov, Yuli Osipovitch Tsederbaum (1873–1923) joined socialist organizations at an early age; at seventeen, he had already distinguished himself as a propagandist among the workers of St. Petersburg. Member of the Workers' Social Democratic Party of Russia, he was on the editorial committee of *The Spark*, along with Lenin. At the Social Democratic Party's Second Congress, Martov led the anti-Leninist faction, thus founding the Menshevik group. After a long period in exile, he returned to Russia after the fall of the Czar in 1917 to head the Mensheviks' internationalist wing, and he strongly condemned the Bolshevik takeover. In 1920, he left Russia again, and died in exile in Germany.

Martov produced numerous theoretical writings, in particular his remarkable *History of Social Democracy in Russia*. In 1919, he outlined the "psychology of Bolshevism" in *Karkov* (Thought), the review of the Social Democratic party.

"What are the defining traits of proletarian Bolshevism as an international phenomenon?

"First of all, a tendency to maximalism, in other words, the will to obtain immediately the most results in the area of social progress, regardless of objective realities. This tendency supposes a strong dose of a naïve social optimism, in its blind faith in the possibility of achieving maximum results at any time, and also in the inexhaustible nature of the resources and goods the proletariat aspires to possess.

"Next, the lack of a serious interest in the realities and necessities of social production, evinced in the priority given, as in the example of the army, to the point of view of the consumer, over that of the producer.

"Finally, the tendency to seek the resolution of political conflicts and power struggles through the immediate recourse to force, even between different segments of the proletariat. This tendency goes hand in hand with a skeptical outlook on democratic solutions to political and social issues.

"The objective conditions that have made these tendencies prevalent in the workers' movement today have already been sufficiently and repeatedly analyzed. The working masses have undergone qualitative change. The mid- and upper-level members of this class have taken their professional qualifications and education to the front, where they have spent four and a half years far from any productive labor and constant appeals to the revolutionary enthusiasm of the masses. Social experimentation soon became impossible, losing its impetus in a maze of chaotic legislation, with decrees often acting at cross-purposes. And yet, proclamations encouraging military discipline and wartime psychology among the workers remained daily fare.

An example of these calls to the population were "communist Saturdays" (*subotnik*), a form of unpaid labor that appeared in several areas of the country as early as the spring of 1919. There

MENSHEVIK EYES

where, penetrated through and through with foxhole psychology, they have lost their soul in a socially amorphous and degraded milieu. Upon their return to the ranks of the proletariat, they brought a revolutionary spirit, but also a spirit of military rebellion. During the war, their places had been taken by millions of fresh workers, ruined craftsmen and other poor devils, country bumpkins and female workers. This new proletariat labored in the absence of a political movement from within itself and could rely only upon the seriously weakened unions. In spite of the increase in industrial output during the war, the German steelworkers' union counted fewer members at the time of the Revolution than in July 1914. The class consciousness of these new workers developed slowly and poorly, and they lacked the experience of organized struggle in collaboration with the higher levels of workers.

"While the masses of men sent to the trenches for years lost their special abilities and the habit of regular, productive labor on the modern, inhuman battlefield, the masses that replaced them were working double time, in order simply to pay the exorbitant price of keeping food on the table. This exhausting labor, accomplished in large part to produce means of destruction, was totally unproductive from a social standpoint. It could certainly not serve to induce in the minds of the workers the consciousness that their labor was indispensable to society's existence—an awareness that is a crucial component of modern proletarian class psychology.

"Bolshevism's rise is based on this context made up of social and psychological factors in every country more or less directly affected by the world war."

Yuli Martov, *World Bolshevism*, Berlin 1923 (Russian edition). ∎

A 10,000 ruble banknote. The plummeting value of the national currency was favorable to the barter economy, which soon replaced commerce entirely. The Bolshevik motto appears in four languages.
Ph © L'Illustration/Sygma

were also "work mobilizations": "weeks" devoted to locomotive repair, distribution, cleaning, or railroad maintenance. People were constantly being summoned to the cry of "Everyone to the labor front!" or the "distribution front." This "front" would be situated in Baku, or on the Donets, or along the Volga. The aim was to spark a multitude of initiatives, to spur the masses to work, as if work could be equated to marching in the streets in a political protest. In the absence of a thought-out plan, rallying cries resounded with revolutionary voluntarism: "Transportation is the key!", "Defeat illiteracy!", "Clean up the streets!", and even "Fight the fleas!"

It is also true, however, that in spite of the chaotic nature of this process, war communism was based on two closely related realities: first, the centralization of political and economic authority, of control over the population and over society, and the substitution of larger economic units for smaller ones, with a rudimentary attempt at national planning; second, the abandonment of commercial and monetary forms of distribution replaced by rationing and free access to

basic goods and services, barter, and payment in kind, and by a system of production more oriented to immediate consumption than to the marketplace.

The integral concentration of the economic system and the disproportionate centralization of political authority, were not simply remedies imposed by civil war on society. They were also the logical consequence of measures envisioned during the pacific phase of the revolution, when it was decided that socialism had to adopt the model of state capitalism (the ultimate stage of concentration and centralization). Also, the elimination of money and the introduction of the "natural" economy reflected an inability to control the conflict between urban and rural areas and resolve the problems of a backward agricultural economy, which affected nearly 80 percent of the population. This policy bore witness to the difficulty in reconciling the anti-feudal rural revolution and the anti-capitalist revolution of the industrial, urban proletariat. Of course, the attempt to "naturalize" the economy went far beyond the capacities of the Bolshevik leaders and called, theoretically as well as practically, for the intervention

Volunteer labor on holidays was first organized by Bolshevik militants in the spring of 1919, on the Moscow–Kazan railroad. It became obligatory for everyone during the "General Labor Mobilization" decreed on January 19, 1920, due to the lack of workers in the cities. Here, a "Communist Saturday" (subotnik) in the city of Chita.
Ph © Keystone

of experts who were in no way concerned by the revolutionary ideology.

From 1921 onward, with the introduction of the New Economic Policy (NEP), war communism would come to a definitive end. The NEP would be based on a rejection of the "natural" economy and the re-establishment of a state-controlled market economy.

The End of the Civil War and Revolts

We can date the start of the transition from war to peace from early 1920, with the defeat of the White Armies of Kolchak, Yudenich, and Denikin.

For about six years, Russians had lived in a state of perpetual war, unceasing social strife, and national conflict. World war, revolution, and civil war had left the people no respite. The October Revolution came hard upon the war between European nations (until the Treaty of Brest-Litovsk) and the conflict opposing the Czarist regime and the Councils (February 1917). The civil war started almost immediately afterward, as did a violent social conflict opposing the "workers' state" and the peasants, who couldn't afford to join the counterrevolutionary cause since they risked renouncing the benefits of agrarian reform. The White Armies' attempt to restore imperial power had further complicated matters by exacerbating highly specific ethnic claims and soliciting the intervention of foreign powers.

Nothing was more urgent than rebuilding the country. The peasants had long awaited the opportunity to exercise their new rights as independent farmers. Factory workers were pressuring the cities, impatient for industrial activity to pick up again. Even the bourgeoisie was expecting to regroup as a legitimate social class, and recover a minimum of economic status. For its part, the Soviet government had regained hope in finally erecting a socialist state in Russia. The transition theory—an idea dear to the moderate wing of the Bolsheviks' first program—made a powerful comeback.

There was also an internal conflict within the Party that had to be resolved without delay, which meant coming to a consensus about whether economic and

We must attach the nucleus of our culture to the precise point where the short and luminous morning of the bourgeois revolution came to an end.

Lunacharski, 1921

social policies that had been implemented until then were simply the result of a form of organization rendered necessary by the conflicts that had lain waste to the country, or if they reflected a coherent and just vision of the path that was to be taken—in other words, the goals espoused by communist doctrine.

It remained to be determined whether war communism was to be pursued, not only through legislation but also through the use of force, or whether another model of development fitted Russia's needs better and its government's aim of bringing the country rapidly to a level of capitalism that Marxist thought considered a prerequisite to socialist experimentation.

In April 1920, Poland invaded the Ukraine. The Red Army, led by General Tukachevski, reacted firmly, and was soon marching toward Warsaw, averting defeat. Once again, war postponed plans for reconstruction, supplying new reasons to adopt ever more radical emergency measures. On October 12, 1920, the Treaty of Riga validated the cessation of hostilities

Red Square, May 5, 1920. Lenin addresses troops on their way to fight the Poles, who had invaded Russia in March. To the right of the podium, Trotsky and Kamenev. In the 1930s, this photograph would be massively reproduced and doctored to eliminate Trotsky and Kamenev, who had both fallen into disgrace.
Ph © Keystone

with Poland. Three weeks later, the last of the counterrevolutionary generals, Baron Piotr von Wrangel, was defeated in the Crimea, and the civil war came to an end with the final victory of the Bolsheviks. Of course, in the south, the anarchist Makhno was still actively harassing Soviet troops. But by November 1920, his army was in tatters and no longer presented a serious threat. What mattered was that Siberia, the Ukraine, and Turkestan had been retaken, with the coal mines of the Donets and the oilfields of Baku. In February 1921, the Red Army succeeded in recovering the Caucasus and entered Tblisi, forcing Georgia's budding Menshevik government out of power. The Soviet regime now controlled a large portion of the former empire. The end of the civil war, coupled with the retreat of Allied forces and the suspension of the economic blockade, opened the way to a new era in Soviet relations with other countries. Diplomatic recognition of the Communist regime and the renewal of trade were imminent.

During the civil war, this propaganda poster by V. Voinov (1920) calls on the Cossacks, who were hostile to the communists, to rally to the Soviet cause: "Now that we're rid of the Czars and the feudal lords, let Cossacks and the working people unite."
Ph © BDIC

Peace did not exactly coincide with the end of war communism's social organization and economic policies. For the moment, the regime sought to perfect a system that had allowed the nation to achieve victory over its foes. The Bolsheviks seemed to envision peace simply as a prolonging of war. During the conflict, they became so used to governing society as a war machine and to considering the successes of its policies as the result of the impeccable functioning of this machine, that the temptation was strong to see communism's future as dependent on the rigorous, systematic implementation of a military plan. Heated debate raged within the Party and the unions, in which opposition groups contested Trotsky and his vision of a militarized labor force.

A WESTERN WRITER IN SOVIET RUSSIA

The British writer H.G. Wells visited Russia in the fall of 1920. Published in the Sunday Express (October 31–November 28, 1920), his impressions, gathered during a two-week stay in Petrograd (with a day in Moscow for a meeting with Lenin), bear witness to the realities of war communism. Wells described the misery of Petrograd, its decimated and starved people, the shops that had closed for lack of merchandise, its ruined streets and houses demolished for firewood. He hid nothing of his concern, not only for Russia's future, but for that of all Europe, if the Allies were to stand by without intervening to stop the collapse of its social and economic system.

"Russia was a modern, Western-style civilization, but the least disciplined and most unstable of the great powers; it is now in its death throes. The direct cause of this catastrophe was modern warfare, which exhausted the country physically. It is these circumstances, and these alone, that allowed the Bolsheviks to seize power. This collapse of Russia is absolutely unprecedented, and, if it continues for another year, it will be irreversible. All that will remain of Russia is a land peopled with savages: cities will be abandoned, in ruins, and the unused railroads will turn to rust. With them, the last vestiges of a central authority will also be annihilated. Peasants are totally illiterate, like an inert mass; capable only of opposing those who seek to meddle in their affairs, they can hardly act with foresight or organize any kind of large-scale venture. They will become a sort of human swamp, the prey of divisions, petty civil wars, and famine as soon as a crop fails. They will be a hotbed of disease for the rest of Europe. And they will swing over to Asia. The ruin of Russian civilization and its peasantry's return to a barbaric state will result, for many years, in Europe no longer having access to its mineral resources, nor other products originating from this country: wheat, linen, etc. We must ascertain whether the Western powers can afford to do without this vast larder. Its disappearance will certainly impoverish Western Europe.

"The only government that might be able to prevent this general collapse is the current Bolshevik government, on the condition that it benefit from American and European aid. There is currently no other alternative. The Bolshevik regime naturally has numerous enemies— adventurers and men of fortune of all sorts—who are ready to work toward its demise with European help, but there are no common goals amongst these people, not the least moral unity that could replace the current authority. Besides, it is no longer the time to foment yet another revolution in Russia. With another year of civil war, this already ruined country will fall for good from the ranks of civilized nations. Willy-nilly, we must come to terms with the Bolshevik regime."

H.G. Wells, *Russia in Shadows*, Paris 1985. ∎

To the Bolsheviks' credit, it should be said that the "dictatorship of distribution" was a positive experience, in that this system of forced requisitions, in spite of its brutality, saved the regime from disintegration, and guaranteed the survival not only of the army, but also of the urban population.

The forced requisitioning from the peasants sounded the death knell of the government's political entente with the peasantry and provoked the inexorable decline of agricultural output. The regime sought to ensure that, now that the war was over, people could be lured back to the cities in order to

The phenomenon of besprizornost, *"abandoned children," had afflicted Russia since well before the Revolution. In 1910, there were approximately 2.5 million* besprizornye, *but that figure that had doubled by 1921. Most of these children lived by begging or petty crime.*
Ph © L'Illustration/Sygma

resume industrial production. Once again asked—in fact, ordered—to give up their harvest, the peasants balked at the renewed requisitions. They fomented revolts, hid their wheat and, in a basic form of rural sabotage, refused to cultivate more than was necessary for their own subsistence. Rural Russia was soon the prey of a new wave of unrest. The most violent revolts broke out in Tambov province, along the middle portion of the Volga, in the Ukraine, in the northern Caucasus, and in western Siberia. These were peripheral zones where the government's power was relatively weak and that possessed a long tradition of popular violence.

Demobilization accelerated the spread of peasant revolts. Hundreds of thousands of soldiers returned to their villages after seven years of war without professions or resources. Many of these spontaneous insurrections took on a more clearly political character. The result was a phenomenon called "banditism," a term that designated various forms of peasant opposition. Often, groups of rebels were made up of socialist revolutionaries or anarchist

CHILDREN AND THE REVOLUTION

Before 1917, the only general legislation concerning child labor was an 1882 law forbidding children under the age of twelve from working in factories; children between the ages of twelve and fourteen were limited to an eight-hour day. Exceptions were numerous, however, and there was no official body in charge of oversight. This allowed factory owners to blithely tell inspectors that "here there are no fixed hours." Child labor was generalized to such an extent that a survey conducted by a group of Moscow teachers revealed that, out of all children of school age, 85 percent of girls and 58 percent of boys under the age of eight were already working.

At the start of the Great War, the 1882 law was repealed. On October 9, 1915, a decree authorized legal minors to work without any restrictions. "Tireless little laborers" flocked to the factories and businesses,

working inhuman hours to compensate for the loss of revenue due to the absence of men at the front. The February Revolution brought the workday down to eight hours, and that of children… to eight hours. There would be no further alterations. This situation provoked a strong reaction among adolescent laborers, who were already politicized. They flooded the press with letters describing how, while adults were marching in the streets, they were locked up, just as in the past, in sweatshops, making boots for women or sewing hems on elegant dresses. True, the 1915 decree was abolished in May 1917, and those under fourteen were barred from working by the end of the summer, but in reality, the situation hardly changed. The decree on the eight-hour workday, published after the October Revolution, instituted a system of protection for female and child labor. The six-hour workday was introduced for fourteen- to

eighteen-year-olds, with no work allowed for younger children; the cut-off age was raised to fifteen on January 1, 1918, and to sixteen exactly one year later. Night shifts and overtime for women and adolescents were also outlawed. However, to enforce these new measures, the Labor Commissariat had to create commissions of inspectors in charge of verifying conformity to the new rules in factories and businesses. In the past, entrepreneurs were opposed to the protection of minors. Henceforth, working parents joined their ranks, unable as they were to make ends meet with their own labor alone. ∎

Heroes of February. The 27,000 sailors of the fort of Kronstadt rebelled on January 28, 1921, with the goal of obtaining better rations, but also new elections. Intent on avoiding the revolt's spreading elsewhere, Bolshevik leaders organized a bloody repression, with at least 1,000 dead and 2,000 wounded among the insurgents.
Ph © Keystone

militants, as well as former members of the armed distribution brigades, those in charge of requisitioning wheat, deserters from the Red Army or work brigades, or former partisans of the counterrevolution. The biggest rebel groups were located without exception in non-industrialized areas. Among the more famous of their leaders were Alexander Antonov (in Tambov and Voronej provinces) and Makhno and Nikolai Grigoriev in the Ukraine.

In the cities too, agitation was rife. Revolts shook Petrograd and Moscow in mid-February 1921, centered on increased food rations, but also on the abolition of military-style labor and the freeing of commerce with rural areas. The aggravation of the social crisis was in large part due to the urban population's utter exhaustion from inhuman labor. The agitation would last three weeks, with strikes, lockouts, massive arrests, and martial law. But they would cease almost as suddenly as they began, without reaching the magnitude of an armed revolt against the state. The Kronstadt revolt best illustrates the difficult situation in which the Soviet regime found itself.

Kronstadt, a fortress and naval base situated on the island of Kotlin about twelve miles from Petrograd, served to protect Petrograd from an invasion by sea. It had become important during the February revolution, with formidable feats of mutiny and pitiless repression and as a model of revolutionary discipline.

In January 1921, Kronstadt held approximately 27,000 sailors and 13,000 workers in charge of the harbor facilities, maintenance of the naval fleet, construction, factories, mills, and electrical installations. Politically, it was a faithful citadel of the regime.

The revolt lasted sixteen days. Begun on January 28, 1921 during a general assembly of sailors, it resulted in the takeover of the fortress without a single shot being fired.

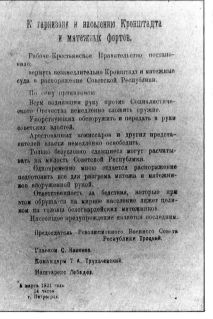

TROTSKY'S TRACT TO THE KRONSTADT REBELS

This proclamation, addressed to the insurgents at Kronstadt, was distributed by airplane over the fortress on March 5, 1921. It was signed by the President of the Military Revolutionary Soviet, Leon Trotsky.

"The government of workers and peasants has established that Kronstadt and the mutinous vessels must immediately be placed at the disposal of the Soviet Republic. To this end, I order: that all those who have raised their hand against the socialist nation immediately lay down their weapons; that those who refuse be disarmed and consigned to the Soviet authorities; that Commissars and other representatives of authority be immediately set free. Only those who surrender will be able to count on the Soviet Republic's clemency. At the same time, I have taken all necessary measures to repress by force this insurrection and all insurgents. The responsibility for the misfortunes that will befall the civilian population lies entirely with the rebellious White Guards. The present warning will be the last." ∎

Ph © L'Illustration/Sygma

Initially, the insurgents demanded better rations and the freedom to trade with the peasants. But the revolt quickly became political, with a call for new elections and for the legalization of all socialist organizations. The official line of the Bolshevik leaders was clear: it was a counterrevolutionary putsch, instigated by the White Guards. The risk of seeing the revolt spread to the workers of Petrograd and the rest of the country, still shaken by the peasant revolts, spurred the regime to a bloody repression of the revolt. Thousands of Communist Party members volunteered under the command of General Tukachevski, and the fortress fell during the night of March 17–18.

The Bolsheviks' refusal to grant any of the rebels' political demands, responding only with repression and purely economic concessions, would mark a

*T*he Red Cavalry enters an Estonian city. General Yudenich's offensive, launched from Estonia on September 8, 1919, brought his counterrevolutionary troops to the suburbs of Petrograd. But the Red Army under Trotsky's command was ultimately victorious. Peace with Estonia was signed on February 2, 1920, followed on July 12 by Lithuania and Latvia on August 11. With these treaties, the Soviet government recognized the independence of the three Baltic nations.
Ph © L'Illustration/Sygma

turning point in the history of the Russian Revolution. In the eyes of many, the military repression of the revolt was an act of unspeakable brutality that definitively buried the myth of a state run by workers, soldiers, and peasants.

Chapter 6

THE NEW
ECONOMIC POLICY

IN 1921, RUSSIA IS STRUCK BY THE WORST FAMINE IN ITS
HISTORY. FACED WITH CATASTROPHE, LENIN ABANDONS WAR
COMMUNISM AND IMPOSES A NEW ECONOMIC POLICY (NEP).

The New Economic Policy, initiated as a new phase of socialist development, reflected a deep crisis within the Soviet regime. In the spring of 1921, the situation was dire. Devastated by war, the situation in the countryside was more serious than the latest harvests, albeit meager, implied. The collapsed rural economy was severely affecting the general economic state of the country. The industrial sector remained obstinately stuck in first gear, and the transportation infrastructure seemed unable to get back on its feet. Goods went undistributed, and there was little hope that things would improve. Entire agricultural regions were threatened with ruin.

In the higher echelons of the Party, everyone was conscious of the threat of "peasant counterrevolution"; Bolshevik leaders tried to understand the implications of the Kronstadt revolt, and were finally learning to heed these menacing signs of the proletariat's exhaustion. It was time for a truce, or rather, an "economic retreat," as the Party would prefer to call it later. This retreat meant above all the abandoning of war communism.

At the very moment that General Tukachevski was marching on Kronstadt, the Tenth Congress of the Communist Party opened in Moscow (March 8–16, 1921). Evoking the end of the "state of emergency," Lenin imposed his New Economic Policy (NEP). The Bolshevik leader admitted that the attempt to achieve a communist

A "propagandamobile" (agitavtomobil) in a demonstration in Leningrad, May 1, 1924. Revolution did not take hold in Western Europe; the New Economic Policy instituted in 1921 was a necessary compromise, a kind of truce between the Soviet regime and the rural population. This turning point provoked contradictory reactions within the Party. Some welcomed it with a feeling of relief; for others, it was a step backward, the beginning of a Russian Winter.
Ph © Coll. part./D.R.

Unemployed workers in front of the Petrograd work exchange. In January 1922, work exchanges posted 160,000 requests for employment to which the stalled Russian economy could not respond.

Ph © Novosti

state had been poorly guided by a simplistic ideology and hastily implemented. Not only a lack of preparation, but the nefarious effects of the protracted war had disrupted distribution circuits almost beyond repair, and industrial production was at a near standstill. The Party had gone too far, and had totally alienated itself from the rural population. Thus the imperative need for an "economic truce."

The End of War Communism

Several distinct social groups had remained excluded from the interests of the revolution: the peasants first and foremost, but also all the workers that had fled the cities during the agrarian reform and the time of industrial paralysis. The new policy change came in answer to the stated priority of recovering these groups by recognizing their role in "revolutionary society." By the end of the war, Russia had become even more rural and peasant-oriented than it had been before. Thus the necessity of a compromise in the construction of socialism, a compromise that, in the tradition of the Second International Communist Movement, was referred to as

a "transition period."

Retreat from policies adopted during war communism was gradual. First, a series of measures was introduced to dismantle the military aspects of civilian existence. These measures would initiate a sequence of events that entailed the reintroduction of a market economy, a new equilibrium of trade between cities and rural areas, and, finally, the injection of money into the economic fabric of the nation. In the countryside, requisitions were definitively abolished, and a certain freedom of trade was the order of the day. This allowed for improved relations with the peasantry and for the implementation of a new agricultural policy.

Moscow, 1922, at the Profintem textile factory. During the civil war years, close links were forged between the different international labor organizations. In 1921, the Profintem, or International Communist Union, was created.
Ph © Novosti

In the cities, minimal conditions for survival had to be achieved to lure workers back to the factories: by 1921, Moscow had lost half its workers and Petrograd had lost two-thirds.

The Tenth Congress of the Bolshevik Party approved the first key policy initiative of the New Economic Policy: taxation in kind (*prodnalog*). This replaced the requisitioning of agricultural surpluses that had been the task of worker brigades, which had provoked dire conflict among different social groups. Peasants were henceforth free to dispose as they saw fit of their surplus, after fulfilling their obligations toward the state. The freeing of trade between urban and rural areas, in spite of numerous restrictions, was meant for peasants and workers to achieve a more harmonious relationship (the "peasant-worker alliance"), without which the Soviet regime could

Opened during the Kronstadt revolt, the Tenth Congress of the Bolshevik Party (March 8–16, 1921) signaled the end of war communism, replaced by the New Economic Policy. Here, Lenin poses surrounded by a group of delegates that had participated in the repression of the revolt.
Ph © Novosti

do nothing about Russia's underdeveloped economy and without which it probably would not survive.

In its theoretical basis, the NEP had few original features. However, seen from the angle of war communism, it struck people's minds as a highly innovative economic proposition. Its fundamental tenet was that agricultural output would increase overall, if peasants were guaranteed the right to trade freely, although within certain limits—that is, a certain freedom of action within the market, coupled with the right to dispose of their own land. This did have a positive effect on the agricultural situation in the short term, with an upsurge in cultivated land and a marked improvement in productivity and yield. However, the measures of 1921 arrived too late to avoid a disastrous famine.

The Famine of 1921

Famine is a phenomenon endemic to Russian history. There were 34 years of penury during the eighteenth century; 40 during the nineteenth (1845–46, 1851, 1855, 1872, 1883, and 1891–92 were the worst years). The beginning of the twentieth century saw an acceleration of this phenomenon, with famines in 1901, 1905, 1906, 1907, 1908, and 1911–12. And the geographic extension of famine was ever-wider: from 1880 to 1890, there were between six and eighteen provinces affected; from 1890 to 1900, from nine to twenty-nine; and from 1901 to 1910, from nineteen to forty-nine, while the 1911–12 famine touched sixty provinces.

The 1921–22 famine, however, was worse than all the others. While the wheat harvest was relatively good in 1920, the following year it reached a mere 38.2 million tons, or half the average pre-war output, with even more catastrophic figures in some regions. A severe drought, for the second year in a row in the eastern provinces of European Russia (in particular the

DEMOGRAPHIC CONSEQUENCES OF THE WAR

At the beginning of the First World War, Russia's population was approximately 171 million. With a death rate of 26.7 percent and a birth rate of 43.7 percent, the total growth rate was 17 percent. Losses during the conflict from 1914–1918 were nearly equivalent to the European average. But Russia would suffer the consequences of a state of war that lasted until the end of 1920, immediately followed by a catastrophic famine. War and the Revolution had a direct influence on the composition and geographical distribution of the population, although the various regions were not affected in the same way by the trauma of war. The European portion of Russia suffered the most from exodus, epidemics, and military mobilization.

During the Great War, the main phenomenon was massive movements of people throughout the country; after the Revolution, this was due to constant evacuations from the various fronts of the civil war. Conscription into the Red and White Armies also had to be taken into account, as well as the journeys undertaken by people illicitly transporting merchandise (meshochnichestvo), the tendency to abandon the cities for the countryside due to the paralysis of the distribution system, and various rural areas abandoned by famine-stricken peasants. Other factors were the economic blockade imposed by the Allied Powers, the scarcity of combustible fuel, the housing crisis, and the lack of essential services in populated areas. ∎

Population of Russia, 1914–1920 58 provinces of European and Asiatic Russia				
			Decrease	
	1914	1920	numbers	percentage
European Russia (Ukraine excluded) (45 provinces)	80,181,520	69,106,006	11,075,514	13.8
Ukraine (2 northern provinces)	4,818,850	4,389,891	428,959	8.9
Total European Russia	**85,000,370**	**73,495,897**	**11,504,473**	**13.5**
Northern Caucasus (3 provinces)	5,641,854	5,335,268	306,586	5.4
Siberia (6 provinces)	10,293,100	9,978,370	314,730	3.1
Kirghiz territory (2 provinces)	1,858,100	1,980,100	82,000	4.4
Total Asiatic Russia	**17,793,054**	**17,293.738**	**703,316**	**3.3**

According to the above data, the population of Russia's 58 European and Asiatic provinces totaled 102,793,424 people at the beginning of this period. In 1920, the census counted 90,789,635 people, which amounts to a decrease of 11.7 percent, or one-ninth of the total population. But geographically, Asiatic Russia lost only one-thirtieth, whereas European Russia lost one-seventh of its population.

The famine of 1921: In the dust-blown streets, starving children look for sunflower seeds. The authorities, slow in realizing the gravity of the situation, attributed the catastrophe to the drought and failed harvests, ignoring the effects of the requisition policy that had stripped rural resources to feed the cities. No fewer than 35 provinces were affected, involving 90,000,000 people.
Ph © L'Illustration/Sygma

grain country of the Volga basin), compounded the effects of a poor harvest. At the end of April, with the announcement of the first measures against the drought, the situation was already serious. In July, the disaster revealed itself to be of unprecedented magnitude. In July, a decree ordered the evacuation of 100,000 people from devastated areas of Siberia. A few days after this decree, it was decided to exempt peasants whose crops had been severely affected from the tax in kind. Thirty-five provinces were affected—approximately 90,000,000 people. Livestock was decimated, for starving peasants all over Russia were killing all their animals for food. Multitudes of men, women, and children took flight in search of less-affected areas in a desperate search for food. The ranks of the *besprizornye*, or abandoned children, a national phenomenon since the civil war, swelled to alarming proportions. In 1922, they numbered five and a half million.

News from famine-stricken areas was dramatic, with cases of insanity, collective suicide, infanticide, and even cannibalism.

The amplitude of the disaster was such that the authorities could no longer hide it or hide from it. The official line faulted only the drought and failed crops, avoiding mention of the requisition policy that had stripped the countryside to feed the cities and more or less directly caused the peasants to plant smaller harvests. The Bolsheviks had no other choice but to request international aid. On August 20, 1921, the Soviet government signed an accord in Riga with the American Relief Administration (ARA), an organization set up by the future American president, Herbert Hoover, to help countries affected by famine. A week later, a similar agreement was signed in Moscow with a representative of the Red Cross, the famous Norwegian explorer Fridtjof Nansen.

The conditions of these accords were humiliating for the Soviets, who were forced to accept on their territory

Faced with unprecedented famine, Bolshevik leaders appealed to the international community and signed an agreement with the American Relief Administration (ARA). The terms of this accord allowed the relief organization to intervene directly to distribute food to the starving. Here, one of its members, in Veselievka.
Ph © L'Illustration/Sygma

private organizations over which they had limited control. A committee for the hungry was also set up in Russia itself (decree of July 21, 1921), with the participation of non-communists such as the economist and statistician Sergei Prokopovitch, former Minister of Distribution under the temporary government of 1917, his wife Catherine Kuskova, and other economists, agronomists, statisticians, doctors, and writers, whose mission was to raise funds in Russia and abroad. This would turn out to be the only attempt in Soviet history at collaboration between members of the government, intellectuals, academics with no party affiliation, and members of other parties. The post of honorary president was given to a renowned writer, Vladimir Korolenko, the only Russian whose moral authority was unanimously recognized. But the committee would not last long. After the accord with the ARA, it was dissolved by the Bolsheviks on August 27, 1921.

During the winter of 1921–22, American and Red Cross contingents worked in the Volga region, which was gripped by both famine and epidemics. The international aid campaign also relied on the collaboration of aid organizations from several other countries. In Berlin, a workers' aid society was founded by Willi Munzenberg; in the US, aid was organized by the Friends of Soviet Russia; in France, a group called Clarté (clarity) was supported by influential personalities such as Anatole France, Henri Barbusse, and Romain Rolland, who mobilized intellectuals. Committees of Friends of Russia were also formed in Germany, Italy, Holland, Norway, Canada, and Australia. In 1922, Nansen would receive the Nobel Peace Prize for his international efforts. Despite these efforts, according to official statistics, at least five million people would die as a result of the 1921–22 famine, with an additional forty million undernourished people.

Market, Exchange, and Trade

Changes in economic policy were to be implemented in a haphazard way. At first, they seemed to be in contradiction with measures that had recently expanded the scope of war communism, for example the decree stating that all goods distributed by the state were henceforth free of

Peasants interviewed by foreign journalists on the reality of famine. The international press took an avid interest in the Russian catastrophe, which it described in graphic detail.
Ph © L'Illustration/Sygma

A LETTER ON FAMINE

This letter by a Slavic specialist, Pierre Pascal, was sent to the *Echo de Paris* on January 16, 1922.

"Maybe when you hear about the famine in Russia, you hear the phrase, 'I'm dying of hunger.' You've never suffered from hunger. Well, here, hunger without such phrases is literally killing men who are your brothers, although they are Russian peasants. Over millions of square miles, nine-tenths of the people have not eaten bread for several months. First, they mixed the remaining flower with all sorts of herbs, then they ate only herbs, then, when nothing else was left, they cooked and ate clay. Now that there is snow on the ground, and people have eaten all the acorns, the diet is now boiled birch bark. Children and the elderly were the first to die. Now, with their last strength, men are digging mass graves—brotherly tombs, they call them—for themselves. The large villages on the Volga, with two or three thousand inhabitants, are seeing 30 people die every day. These figures are repre-sentative of the general situation. There are cases of cadavers exhumed and eaten, mothers leaving their children in the forest or throwing them in the river to escape this horrible temptation. I don't want to think these cases are part of a general tendency. But every day, until the next harvest, the circle of death will grow wider, with more and more districts and areas where nothing humanly edible will remain."

Pierre Pascal, *The State of My Soul: A Journal of Russia*, Vol. 3 (1922–1926), Lausanne 1982. ∎

The Prokorov factory cooperative, 1920. The organization of trade under the NEP was divided into three areas: the private sector prevailed in the exchange of retail goods; cooperatives operated on both a wholesale and a retail basis; and state organizations traded in wholesale merchandise.
Ph © Harlingue-Viollet

charge (October 11, 1920) and the bill suppressing taxes and monetary contributions (February 3, 1921). But this contradiction was only superficial, for in this first phase of transition, the Soviet government did not intend to renounce completely the principles of a "natural" economy. Free trade in goods was strictly limited to localized areas (the provinces) and it had to take the form of barter (agricultural goods for industrial products).

Under the pressure of the economic situation, which was developing extremely rapidly, the authorities were forced to legalize the reconstitution of markets and to give juridical form to monetary circulation in the country. Thus, the tax in kind soon became a money tax. The NEP as an economic policy had to promote trade and the circulation of goods. On the financial level, it was obvious that the Peoples' Commissars and the board of directors of the state bank had to abandon their inflationist strategy, ensure a stable currency, and guarantee the rapid circulation of money. From the summer of 1921 onward the first steps were taken to build a modern

system of credit. It quickly proved impossible to limit the scope of the NEP to local commerce, and prevent the use of money in trade between the industrial and agricultural sectors, given that consumers were regaining confidence in the ruble.

The Bolsheviks, in fact, were learning about the most elementary laws of the market and about the repercussions the market economy has on society as a whole. Trade relationships typical of a capitalist system were developing at breakneck speed in several major sectors of the national economy. The growth of local trade contributed to the development of the national market, and resulted in the disappearance of barter. The private sector included henceforth not only farmers, but also artisans and small businesses. Other measures gave more impetus to the phasing out of the barter economy: services such as housing, water, electricity, and gas were no longer free, and payment was reintroduced for transportation, the postal service, and newspapers. This "liberalization" affected a vast set of goods that were until then at the charge of the state. In the second half of 1921, almost all salaries were paid in currency. The cycle of war communism was effectively at an end.

At the same time as radical reforms were being initiated in agricultural policy that aimed to ensure the peasantry's adhesion to the NEP, Bolshevik leaders

Advertisement for Mozer watches, sold in the GUM (Universal State Stores), the largest chain of retail outlets, with branches throughout the country. Within the context of a much-desired increase in productivity, watches became an item of mass consumption in the early 1920s: "Man—only with a watch. Watches—only from the Mozer factories. Mozer watches—only at GUM."
Ph © Documentation Leclanche-Boulé

were busy forging a new industrial policy. They referred back to the organizational model of state capitalism, back to the first days of the Revolution. The envisioned system included four main areas of action. The first took the form of concessions, with the state granting foreign capitalists a role in businesses over which it retained control. The second instituted co-operation between manufacturers. The third consisted in paying a percentage-based commission on goods purchased from small manufacturers and then resold to the State. And the fourth form of state capitalism was based on the rental of nationalized industries and institutions belonging to the state, cooperatives, or private individuals who thus obtained the right to exploit mineral resources and the vast forested domains.

The rebirth of trade went hand in hand with the reappearance of the national currency, which economic leaders attempted to stabilize from 1921 onward. Here, Nikolai Brukanov, the Deputy Commissar of Finance, displays newly-minted coins (10, 15, 20, and 50 kopecks and the one-ruble coin.
Ph © Coll. Viollet

At right: Selling soup in the streets of Petrograd.
Ph © L'Illustration/Sygma

But Russia still lagged economically; workers numbered only two and a half million, against 110 million peasants. Industrial centers were few, like islands in an ocean of small farms. In the words of the economist Vladimir Bazarov, these were in essence "historical museums that bore witness to the evolution of Russian industry from the seventeenth century to today." Moreover, "representation was disproportionately in favor of the seventeenth and eighteenth centuries, rather than the nineteenth." In such a context, how was productivity to be raised? This remained the sine qua non condition of the edification of a socialist system.

The first measures adopted in industry also

THE NEP ACCORDING TO A FEMALE BOLSHEVIK MILITANT

In her memoirs, Elizabeth Drabkina, one of the original Bolsheviks and a participant in the repression at Kronstadt, bears witness to the concerns that the turnabout of 1921 elicited among communist militants. Although the NEP aimed to surmount the hostility between the urban proletariat and the peasantry, it gave rise to a far less noble reality, a sort of "black-market NEP" that could be observed in the streets of Moscow.

"Look at what's happening in Moscow… The great Russian historian Vassily Ossipovitch Klyuchevski compared historical turning points to the effects of a storm: in the same way that the tempest blasts through the trees, showing the underside of the leaves, historical turning points turn the life of a people upside down. This is what occurred at the beginning of the NEP. Where did it come from? Where to find its source? The vibrant, indestructible Sukarevka (Moscow black market) existed before and was renowned throughout Russia. In spite of interdictions, repeated raids on the market, it was like plunging a knife into gelatin. But hardly had the laws implementing the new order been promulgated—the term "new economic policy" had not yet come into use—but like dough that had been left to rise too long and starts to ferment, there appeared hordes of profiteers, currency traffickers, speculators, pawn shops, shady intermediaries, swindlers, and other types of sharks. […] These characters were shouting, sweating, carrying sacks from one train station to another, gathering under railroad bridges, invading the Zatsepa, the Trubnaya and the Sukarevka

It was a veritable tower of Babel, a human tidal wave, with dangerous eddies and whirlpools, a loud, frenetic horde, chewing sunflower seeds, swearing at God, the Devil, the Saints and your entire family […].

The Sukarevka? Food fit for pigs! But look at Okotny Riad: opposite the Moskva Hotel, a double row of boutiques and stalls—selling meat, cold cuts, cheese, dairy products, fruits, and vegetables—has sprouted right out of the ground, an imposing double wall of merchants facing both the sidewalk and the street.

And such an assortment of delicacies! Goods for gourmets, cultivated and shipped with the utmost care. Every cheese is perfectly ripe. Caviar like red and black pearls. Ham that you would swear was pink satin. Where can all these treasures come from in this barren, exhausted, starving country? In what hidden lair had they lain all these years, this merchant counting on his abacus, those beady eyes shining out of a greasy face, fat like a full moon, peering out of the shadows of his boutique?"

Elizabeth Drabkina, *Winter Solstice: Lenin's Last Fight*, Les Editeurs Français Réunis, Paris 1970. ∎

A suburban train in Moscow, overflowing with demobilized soldiers, peasants fleeing famine, and workers going back to their former jobs, repopulating the cities after years of war.
Ph © L'Illustration/Sygma

contributed to the dismantling of war communism. Factories could no longer be nationalized without previous deliberation by the highest administrative echelons, work brigades were abolished, workers could choose to work wherever they wished; and salaries were no longer strictly egalitarian, but henceforth based on productivity. There was much emphasis laid on the fact that free trade and better wages would encourage workers to take more interest in the fruits of their labor and improve production methods. The resolution on the role of the unions, approved by the Tenth Party Congress, proposed a wage policy still based on equal compensation for all industrial workers. But a decree passed on April 7, 1921 instituted bonuses paid in kind: in several sectors of industry, higher productivity was rewarded by a certain quantity of products from the factory, that workers then used in direct trade with peasants.

Debate raged in the press on issues such as

worker productivity and mass psychology. It was observed that the drop in productivity, from the February Revolution to well after the October Revolution, was not only due to material causes. While the Revolution did in fact disrupt the habits of the masses, weakening their will to work and deforming their ideas about services they now felt entitled to receive for free, it was the leveling of wages—with the rejection of all forms of remuneration linked to the quantity or quality of work—that in fact generated the collapse of productivity. In 1923, after the adoption of rigorous measures dealing with the reorganization of factories on the basis of auto-financing (*kozraschet*), industrial trusts were set up, functioning on their own responsibility and on a commercial basis, in order to obtain profits. The Soviet trusts would be totally independent in the management of their economic interests, while state organizations retained general control and oversight of their activities.

In the place of your hopes of yesterday, in the cafés stuffing themselves with pastry until they're sick, the petit bourgeois are there, glorifying communism.

Mayakovsky, 1922

ПРОЛЕТАРИИ

Project for Lenin's tribune (1924) by the constructivist architect, Eliezar Lissitzki. "Constructivism" promoted the creative freedom of the artist with respect to traditional techniques. Lissitzki's project, which was never realized, is depicted in this photomontage: Lenin's silhouette, leaning out of the tribune, was added to the model to give a dynamic thrust to the image.
Ph © Coll. part./D. R.

The effects of the New Economic Policy were remarkable. The decline in productivity leveled off, then, at a gradually increasing pace, began to rise again. Economic reconstruction in industry was achieved in an irregular fashion, but its effects were global, touching various sectors according to need. Heavy industry (energy, metallurgy) was attended to a short time after light industry (textiles, tractors, trucks, automobiles), manufacturers of consumer goods, and food products. In 1924, these two sectors accounted for two-thirds of global industrial output. In general, the process of reconstruction aimed to reestablish the proportions and relationships prevalent in the different branches of the economy before the war.

In the agricultural sector, the most important advances concerned the extension of cultivated areas, livestock, increasing overall yield, and improving nutrition in the population as a whole. In the interests of reconstruction, it was necessary to facilitate the influx of foreign capital in all areas of the economy, either in the form of concessions or as borrowed funds. Certain denationalized industries were allowed to trade with individual interests, and trade delegations were sent abroad.

Throughout this entire venture, the rallying cry was the transformation of the workforce, of its capacities and its awareness. "Socialism" seemed no longer the "political" affair of the workers, but simply a question of productivity.

Crisis in the Party

"Nepmen" was the name given to those who were most able to take advantage of the liberalization of the market and the "privatization" of the economy. Indeed, the Nepmen were the protagonists of a new form of a mixed economy, characterized by the predominance of

agriculture over industry, and by the legalization of trade and small businesses.

The private sector flourished, mostly in the form of small businesses run by individuals or families (most employed fewer than ten people). Free commerce filled in the gaps left by state distribution and cooperatives. It was only from 1923 onward that the state succeeded in improving its own distribution capacity and in recovering a significant portion of its control over the market, first through traditional mechanisms such as competition, then by adopting repressive measures against the Nepmen.

It would be mistaken to suppose that the Soviet government had chosen to revert to the pure economic liberalism espoused by those segments of the old bourgeoisie that had attempted to collaborate with the

The First Congress of the USSR (December 30, 1922) approved the treaty of union between the socialist federal republics of Russia, the Ukraine, Belarus, and Transcaucasia. The Congress of Soviets was the supreme body of authority in the USSR; directly beneath were the pan-Russian organizations, which exercised jurisdiction over all Soviet territory. It was headed by a Central Executive Committee (CIK).
Ph © Novosti

*L*enin in his study at Gorky, in
August 1922. Following a
cerebral hemorrhage in May, the
Bolshevik leader's condition was
grave. In his last notes, referred
to as his "testament," he
denounced the risks of a schism
within the Party, due to the rivalry
between Stalin and Trotsky.
Ph © Keystone

regime. Liberalism was limited to precisely defined sectors of the economy with the state remaining the primary economic entity, even under the NEP. It kept a firm grip on heavy industry, foreign and national trade, and on the banking and credit system. Opposed to the creation of large private industry, it also retained control over most of the manufacturing and mining sectors.

The "retreat of communism" provoked intense and contradictory reactions. The non-communist press spoke out in its favor, and saluted the NEP as a long-awaited opportunity to revive a free interplay of all the economic, political, and ideological currents that had lain dormant in Russia. On their side, the Bolshevik cadres and leaders took comfort in the change of perspective, sharing the belief that there was no viable alternative capable of building a socialist economy. At the grassroots level of the Party, however, there was disappointment and confusion. Communism seemed to recede endlessly over the horizon. Was NEP a capitulation to capitalism, a retreat into the comfort zone of the bourgeois revolution? For them, the October Revolution might have been a grand illusion.

During the civil war, party membership had grown

considerably, from around 200,000 at the end of 1917 to 750,000 in March 1921. But after the introduction of the New Economic Policy, thousands of communists left the Party. The Communist Youth Organization (Komsomol) lost almost half of its members in two years; there was even an epidemic of suicides in its ranks. In the view of many militants, the NEP was nothing but a reformist derivative, and the Nepmen, profiteers and speculators.

Lenin's funeral, January 27, 1924. For hours, crowds paid their respects to the Bolshevik leader, whose coffin was exposed on Red Square. The previous day, five days after the death of the hero of the October Revolution, the city of Petrograd changed its name to Leningrad. Ph © L'Illustration/Sygma

The Party had been through its first serious internal crisis in 1919–20, with the formation of several opposition factions and groups criticizing the administration's authoritarian management of the economy and bureaucratic excesses within the Party. For example, there were the "democratic centralists" (N. Osinski, Timothy Sapronov, and V. Smirnov), and the "workers' opposition" (Alexander Chliapnikov, L. Lutovinov, Sergei Medvedev, and Alexandra Kollontai). Controversy centered notably on the role of the unions. During this period, the Party resolutely embarked on the path to centralization. This process would culminate after the state of emergency had ended.

Lively debate and heated political conflict reflected

Mikhail Kalinin (1875–1946), a peasant revolutionary, was nominated president of the Central Executive Committee of the Soviets by Lenin, because of his knowledge of the rural world. He would occupy this important post—equivalent to President of the Republic—until his death. His wife was arrested during the purge of 1937, and he would remain the hostage of Stalin, his immense prestige providing a "cover" for Stalin's policies.
Ph © L'Illustration/Sygma

the vitality of internal opposition. In the autumn of 1920, the Party barely managed to navigate between the Scylla and Charybdis of the far-left and the anti-communist rebellion. This was a critical period in the struggle against political representatives of the "workers' opposition," whose platforms were clearly inspired by the disappointment of the worker elite with the first measures preceding the NEP. The opposition refused to renounce the principle of total worker control over factory management and industrial production; indeed, workers were being asked to content themselves with "political" control and an "accountant's" role in this sector. It firmly condemned the discarding of communist experimentation and the rise to prominence of experts, technicians, and non-Party administrators.

In 1921, the NEP sought to impose rigorous unity and strict discipline within the Party. The Tenth Congress was decisive in the history of the Bolshevik organization. The need for cohesion being recognized, the Congress approved the interdiction and immediate dissolution of the factions (with two motions in particular: "On syndicalist and anarchist deviation within the Party" and "On Party unity"). The freedom to criticize policies was brutally stigmatized as conducive to "disease." Firm repression of left-wing opposition was in fact the counterpart to the compromise with non-communists within the production sectors.

The disagreements, hesitations, and soul-searching elicited by the NEP among the militants nevertheless led the Bolshevik leaders to step up their efforts to centralize the Party. This entailed renouncing for good a certain kind of broad collaboration and a different political harmony. The monopoly over power would be validated by the adoption of a one-party system in Soviet Russia. From then on, the Russian Communist Party became the sole legal political organization in the country, and representatives of other groups would be reduced to silence, arrested, tried, and expelled; during the summer of 1922, the trial of socialist revolutionaries would become notorious even abroad.

A few days after the end of the Eleventh Party Congress (late March–early April 1922) two major events occurred. On April 4, the newspaper Pravda

published—in a few lines—a news item that would go almost unnoticed: "The Central Committee elected by the Eleventh Congress of the Russian Communist Party has confirmed its secretariat, to wit the following: comrade Stalin (First Secretary), comrade Molotov, and comrade Kubichev." The Central Committee was henceforth headed by one Secretary, aided by two assistants, and no longer by three secretaries at the same level. With the creation of the post of Secretary General, the principle of collective authority at the summit of the party hierarchy was definitively abandoned.

On May 25, 1922, at the age of 52, Lenin was struck by a cerebral hemorrhage and remained paralyzed on one side. From this day until his death, on January 21, 1924—except for short periods in the autumn and winter of 1922–23—he was forced to cease all political activity. This opened the way for the rise to power of Stalin.

From left to right: Stalin, Rykov, Kamenev, Zinoviev. Rykov took over the presidency of the Sovnarkom (the Council of People's Commissars) from Lenin, while the party executive passed into the hands of the Troika, Stalin-Zinoviev-Kamenev, allied in the fight against Trotsky.
Ph © L'Illustration/Sygma

THE BIRTH
OF THE USSR

VICTORIOUS IN THE CIVIL WAR, THE BOLSHEVIKS CREATE THE
USSR, RESUSCITATING THE OLD EMPIRE. BASED ON THE FREE
CONSENT OF THE EMPIRE'S PEOPLES, THE NEW REGIME WOULD
DURABLY SUSPEND NATIONAL CLAIMS.

The Great War signaled the end of three great empires that rose and fell with the advent of modern times: Austria-Hungary, Imperial Russia, and the Ottoman Empire. It had been a long-term process, begun in the nineteenth century with the slow but sure erosion of the peripheral territories of these empires. With the Great War over, the different nations included in these three aggregates of multi-ethnic peoples severed their ties with the political authority that had united them until then, and validated this break by declaring independence. The birth of Finland as well as that of Poland (and the three Baltic States), the reconstitution of Georgia, Armenia, and Bessarabia seemed to partake of the same logic as Hungary, Czechoslovakia, and Yugoslavia, all newly-formed entities—and the new affirmation of the Arab world.

But in Russia, this breakaway process of nations within an empire, after having been legitimized during the October Revolution with the proclamation of the rights of peoples—equality and sovereignty—came up against contrary forces, and ended up being inverted. Revolutionary movements sprang up at the heart of secessionist nationalisms, and, in order to vanquish bourgeois proponents of self-determination, their leaders were forced to become the allies of the Soviets, who alone could guarantee the dictatorship of the

Moscow's fortified heart, the Kremlin dominates the left bank of the Moskova. Former residence of the Czars, it consists of several administrative edifices and churches. From 1918, the Senate palace became the seat of power of the Soviet government.
Ph © L'Illustration/Sygma

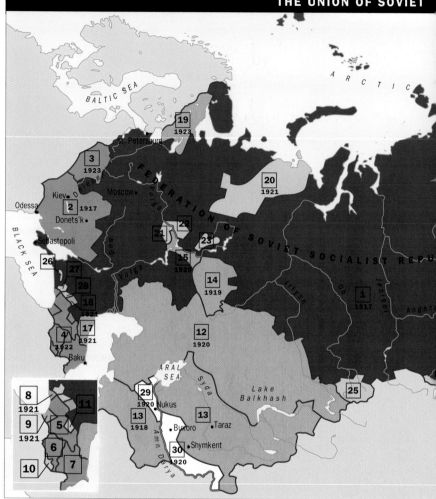

proletariat at a local level. Just as the Bolsheviks refused to renounce the former boundaries of the empire in the name of self-determination, the revolutionary elite in the various republics could not deny the Soviet government's status as a natural partner in a federative system. This was what distinguished the Russian situation from the collapse of the Austro-Hungarian or Ottoman Empires: the October Revolution suspended and blocked the movements of national liberation initiated during the

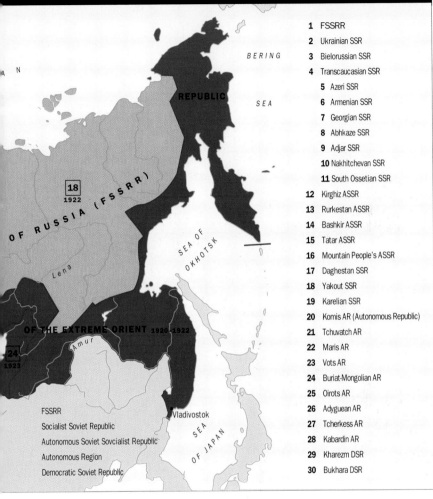

#	
1	FSSRR
2	Ukrainian SSR
3	Bielorussian SSR
4	Transcaucasian SSR
5	Azeri SSR
6	Armenian SSR
7	Georgian SSR
8	Abhkaze SSR
9	Adjar SSR
10	Nakhitchevan SSR
11	South Ossetian SSR
12	Kirghiz ASSR
13	Rurkestan ASSR
14	Bashkir ASSR
15	Tatar ASSR
16	Mountain People's ASSR
17	Daghestan SSR
18	Yakout SSR
19	Karelian SSR
20	Komis AR (Autonomous Republic)
21	Tchuvatch AR
22	Maris AR
23	Vots AR
24	Buriat-Mongolian AR
25	Oirots AR
26	Adyguean AR
27	Tcherkess AR
28	Kabardin AR
29	Kharezm DSR
30	Bukhara DSR

Legend on map:
FSSRR
Socialist Soviet Republic
Autonomous Soviet Sovcialist Republic
Autonomous Region
Democratic Soviet Republic

nineteenth century all over Europe, a movement that bore fruit after the First World War.

During the civil war, Soviet Russia was essentially composed of the Federated Soviet Socialist Republic of Russia (FSSRR), representing 92 percent of the former empire's territory and 70 percent of its population. Its first Constitution dates from July 1918, and bilateral accords linked it with other Soviet Republics (Ukraine, Belarus, the three republics of the Caucasus, the Far-East Republic, and the two Central

Asian republics). At the end of the civil war, it was generally recognized that the time had come to consolidate and deepen ties that, during the hostilities, had taken a military form.

How would this reunification occur at the same time as the birth of a new state, a new kind of empire that no one had foreseen only a few years before?

First, through the restoration of the three Slavic peoples (Great Russians, Ukrainians, and White Russians), who accounted for about four-fifths of the former empire. In this context, the formal supremacy of Moscow was reestablished, as was the centralizing influence of the Great Russians who were to keep the reins of industrial and economic power. The process of unification coincided with the birth of a Soviet Russian patriotic sentiment. Contrary to the counterrevolutionary governments, which were seeking and obtaining the support of foreign powers, the Red Army was seen by local populations as a guarantee against national dismemberment.

Then, the Soviets sought to give this union a democratic ideological foundation, by recognizing the right to secede, the right to self-determination, and the principle of free association of all members. By the end of 1922, the process of unification was all but complete. On December 20, 1922, the First Congress of the Soviets of the USSR approved the treaty of union between the Socialist Federated Republics of Russia (capital, Moscow), the Ukraine (capital, Karkov), Belarus (capital, Minsk) and the Transcaucasus (capital Tlibissi). In the words of Stalin's inaugural address to the Congress: "It is the victory of the New Russia over the Old Russia, over the 'policeman of Europe' and the 'butcher of Asia'."

A solemn declaration fixed the formal principles of union between the republics ("the pacific coexistence and fraternal collaboration of peoples"), and also explained the economic, military, and ideological reasons behind this union:

"Razed fields, paralyzed factories, productive forces annihilated, and economic resources exhausted—this is the legacy of war, which dooms in advance the isolated Republics' attempts at economic reconstruction.

The rebuilding of the economy will be impossible if the Republics remain separated.

"Moreover, the instability of the international situation and the threat of new aggression make the formation of a unified front of Soviet Republics necessary to break capitalist encirclement.

"Lastly, the very structure of Soviet power, which is by nature international due to its basis in the class struggle, impels the masses of workers toward unification within a single socialist family.

"The above circumstances call imperiously for the edification of the Soviet Republics in a Federative State, capable of guaranteeing security from foreign powers, economic growth within its borders, and the free growth its nations and peoples."

After the declaration of July 6, 1923, the Soviet State was officially consecrated as the Union of Soviet Socialist Republics (USSR). The Fundamental Law promulgated on January 31, 1924 embodied the ideal reconciling of the dictatorship of the proletariat and the nationalities. It even foresaw the advent of a worldwide USSR. This Constitution would undergo several modifications (in particular the Constitution of December 5, 1936), but it would accompany the USSR until its last moments.

During the perestroika years, the crisis in which the USSR was plunged seemed to have been marked by the same ferments of dissolution that had undermined the empires of the nineteenth century. The disappearance of the USSR heralded the belated coming of age of its many nations. Faced with a greatly weakened central authority, the right to secede and the right to self-determination were finally invoked, as stipulated in the Constitution of 1923—as if seventy years of socialism had only suspended the ineluctable evolution of history.

Bibliography

■ General Works
Goody, J. *Socialism in Russia: Lenin and His Legacy, 1890–1991*. New York: Palgrave Macmillan, 2002.
Pipes, R. The Russian Revolution. New York: Vintage, 1997 (reprint).
Seton-Watson, H. *The Russian Empire (1801–1917)*. Oxford: Oxford University Press, 1967.

■ Lenin
Lenin, V.I. *"What is To Be Done?" and Other Writings*. New York: Dover Publications, 1987.
Service, R. *Lenin: A Biography*. Cambridge: Belknap Press, 2002.
Volkogonov, D. *Lenin: A New Biography*. New York: Free Press, 1994.

■ Parties and Revolutionary Movements
Daniels, R. V. *The Conscience of the Revolution: Communist Opposition in Soviet Russia*. Cambridge: Harvard University Press, 1960.
Haimson, L.H. *The Mensheviks: from the Revolution of 1917 to the Second World War*. Chicago: University of Chicago Press, 1974.
Rosenberg, W.G. *Liberals in the Russian Revolution: The Constitutional Democratic Party, 1917–1921*. Princeton: Princeton University Press, 1974.

■ Revolution and the Soviet State
Carr, E.H. *The Interregnum, 1923–24*. London: Macmillan, 1954.
Hasegawa, T., *The February Revolution: Petrograd 1917*. Seattle: University of Washington Press, 1981.
Remnick, D. *Lenin's Tomb: The Last Days of the Soviet Empire*. New York: Vintage, 1994.

■ The Civil War and War Communism
Benvenuti, F. *The Bolsheviks and the Red Army, 1918–1922*. Cambridge, UK: Cambridge University Press, 1987.
Koenker D., Rosenberg W. and Suny G. (eds.) *Party, State and Society in the Russian Civil War*. Bloomington: Indiana University Press, 1989.
Mawdsley, E. *The Russian Civil War*. Boston: Unwin Hyman, 1987.
Malle S. *The Economic Organization of War Communism, 1918–1921*. Cambridge: Cambridge University Press, 1985.

Chronology

All events are dated according to the Julian calendar that Russia used until February 1, 1918, when the modern Gregorian calendar was adopted. The Julian calendar is thirteen days behind; events are given in the Gregorian calendar in parentheses.

1898   **March 1–3** (13–15): First Congress of the Workers Social-Democratic Party (WSDP) in Minsk.

1901   **November–December:** Unification of populist factions in the Socialist Revolutionary Party.

1903   **July 17–August 10** (July 30–August 23): Second Congress of the WSDP in Brussels and London. Formation of the two opposing groups, Bolsheviks and Mensheviks.

1904   **January 26–27** (Feburary 8–9): War breaks out between Russia and Japan.

1905   **January 3 (16):** The Putilov factories go on strike in St. Petersburg. **January 9** (22): "Bloody Sunday" in St. Peterburg; bloody repression of a massive demonstration (140,000 participants). **April 12–27** (April 25–May 10): Third Congress of the WSDP in London. **May 15** (28): Creation of the first soviet at Ivanovo Voznesenk. **August 6** (19): Manifesto announcing the creation of a chamber of deputies (the Duma). **August 23** (September 5): Treaty of Portsmouth ending the Russian-Japanese War. Russia loses Port Arthur, the Southern Manchurian railroad, and the southern portion of the island of Sakhalin. **October 12–18** (25–31): Foundational congress of the Constitutional Democratic Party (Cadets). **October 13** (26): Foundation of the St. Petersburg soviet. **October 17** (30): October Manifesto establishing civil rights. **November 10** (22): Formation of the Octobrist Party (or Union of October 17). **November 22** (December 5): Foundation of the Moscow soviet. **December 8–18** (21–31): General Strike and insurrection in Moscow.

1906   **April 24–27** (May 7–10): The First Duma is convened.

1907   **February 20** (March 5): The Second Duma is convened. **April 30–May 19** (May 13–June 1): Fifth Congress of the WSDP in London. **November 1 (14):** The Third Duma.

1912   **November 15** (28): The Fourth Duma.

1914   **July 18** (31): General mobilization of Russian armies. **July 19** (August 1): Germany declares war on Russia. **July 24** (August 6) Austria-Hungary declares war on Russia. **August 4** (17): Start of the Russian offensive in eastern Prussia. **August 5** (18): Start of the Russian offensive in eastern Galicia.

1917   **February 9** (22): Demonstration in Petrograd to commemorate Bloody Sunday of 1905. **February 18** (March 3): Start of the Putilov strike in Petrograd. **February 23** (March 8): International Women's Day. Thousands of women and workers march in the streets of Petrograd. **February 25** (March 10): General strike in Petrograd. First violent clashes between soldiers and demonstrators. **February 26** (March 11): Violence erupts; the army kills 150 people. First desertions. State of siege declared in

1917 Petrograd. Appeal of the Duma President, Mikhail Rodzianko, for the formation of a "Ministry of Confidence." **February 27** (March 12): February Revolution. Mutinies in several regiments. Occupation of the Fortress of Peter and Paul, of the Arsenal, and of the Winter Palace by soldiers and workers. **March 2** (15): Accord between the Committee of the Duma and the Soviet. Formation of a temporary government with a liberal majority. Abdication of Nikolai II. **March 7** (20): The temporary government issues a warrant for the Czar's arrest. **March 11** (24): France, Italy, and Great-Britain recognize the temporary government. **March 25** (April 7): State monopoly on cereal products. **April 3** (16): Lenin returns from exile to Petrograd. **April 4** (17): The April Theses expound communism in ten principles. **May 4** (17): Trotsky returns from exile. **June 3–24** (June 16–July 7): First Congress of the Soviets of Deputies of Workers and Soldiers, in Petrograd. **July 3–5** (16–18): "Days of July" in Petrograd. Failure of an uprising of soldiers, sailors, and workers, supported by the Bolsheviks. **July 8** (21): Kerenski is made Prime Minister of the temporary government. **July 26–August 3** (August 8–16): Sixth Congress of the WSDP. **August 25–31** (September 7–13): Kornilov attempts a coup. **September 9** (22): Trotsky is elected President of the Petrograd Soviet. **October 10** (23): A secret meeting of the Bolshevik Party's Central Committee approves a plan for armed insurrection. **October 12** (25): Formation of a Revolutionary Military Committee, under the Petrograd Soviet, commanded by Trotsky. **October 24–25** (November 7–8): Second Congress of Soviets. Formation of the Sovnarkom (Council of Commissars of the People) led by Lenin. Decrees on Peace and Land. **November 2** (15): Declaration on the rights of the peoples of Russia. **November 3** (16): Victory of the Bolshevik insurrection in Moscow. **November 14** (27): Decree on worker control. **December 2** (15): Armistice declared with the Axis Powers (Germany, Austria-Hungary, Bulgaria, and Turkey). Creation of the Vesencha (High Council on the National Economy). **December 7** (20): Foundation of the Tcheka (Extraordinary Commission for the Struggle against the Counterrevolution and Sabotage). **December 14** (27): Banks are nationalized.

1918 **January 5** (18): A Constituent Assembly is convened in Petrograd with a majority of Socialist Revolutionaries. **January 6** (19): The Constituent Assembly is dissolved by order of the Soviet Central Executive Committee. **January 7–14** (20–27): First Pan-Russian Congress of Unions. **January 15** (28): Creation of the Red Army of Workers and Peasants. **January 10–18** (23–31) Third Congress of Soviets proclaiming the Soviet Socialist Federated Republic of Russia (SSFRS). **January 21** (February 3): The new Republic cancels all its domestic and foreign debts. **February 1** (14): The Gregorian calendar is adopted. **March 3**: The Treaty of Brest-Litovsk is signed with the Central Powers. **March 6-8**: Seventh Congress of the WSDP, which now calls itself the Russian Communist (Bolshevik) Party. **March 12**: The capital is transferred from Petrograd to Moscow. **March 14–16**: Fourth Congress of the Soviets. **May 13**: The Commissariat for Distribution arrogates extraordinary powers to requisition; the "dictatorship of distribution." **May 25**: The Czechoslovak Legion revolts. **June 8**: Formation of the Constituents' Committee of Samara (Komutch). **June 11**: Organization of committees of poor peasants (*kombedy*) in opposition to the kulaks. **June 28**: Big industries are nationalized. **July 4–10**: Fourth Congress of Soviets. **July 6**: Revolt of left-wing revolutionary socialists.

1918 The German ambassador, Count von Mirbach, is assassinated. **July 10**: First Soviet Constitution. **Night of July 16–17** Execution of the Czar, Nikolai II, and his family at Ekaterninenburg. **August**: High point of the White Army offensive along the Volga. **August 30**: Lenin survives an attempt on his life in Moscow. Assassination of Uritski, President of the Petrograd Tcheka. **September 8–23**: Conference of Ufa, uniting governments, parties, and organizations hostile to the Bolsheviks. Creation of a temporary government at Omsk. **December 10**: Publication of the Code of Law governing work and workers.

1919 **March 2–6**: First Congress of the Komintern (International Communist Party) in Moscow, with 52 delegates from 30 countries. **March 18–23**: Eighth Congress of the Communist Party. March: Kolchak leads his troops toward Simbirsk and Samara. April: Counteroffensive of the Red Army against Kolchak. **April 12**: First "Communist Saturday" (subotnik) organized by workers of the Moscow-Kazan railroad. **May–September**: Iudenitch launches an offensive toward Petrograd, while Denikin pushes to the Ukraine, the Volga, and Moscow. **October**: Counteroffensive of the Red Army against Iudenitch and Denikin. **November 14**: Occupation of Omsk by the Bolsheviks; Kolchak retreats to Irkutsk.

1920 **January 15**: Definitive dissolution of Kolchak's government in Siberia. **January 29**: Decree on the obligation to work. **February 7**: Kolchak is executed at Irkutsk. **March 29–April 5**: Ninth Congress of the Communist Party. **April–September**: War against Poland. **June**: Offensive of General Wrangel in the Ukraine. **July 19–7**: August II Komintern Congress. **October 12**: Armistice with Poland at Riga. **November:** The Bolsheviks are victorious against Wrangel. End of the civil war. **November–March 1921**: Controversy over trade unions. **December 22–29**: Eighth Congress of the Soviets.

1921 **February**: Worker agitation in Petrograd and Moscow. **February 22**: Creation of the Gosplan (Commission for General Planning). **February 25**: The Menshevik government in Georgia is overthrown. **February 28–March 18**: Kronstadt Revolt. **March 8–16**: Tenth Congress of the Communist Party. Beginning of the New Economic Policy (NEP). **March 16**: Trade agreement with Great Britain. **March 21**: Decree on taxation in kind. **March 28**: Decree allowing free commerce in agricultural products. **May 6**: Temporary trade agreement with Germany. **June 22–July 12**: Third Komintern Congress. **July 21**: Creation of a Committee to Help the Starving. **August 20**: Accord between the Soviets and the American Relief Organization (ARA) to fight the famine. **Summer–autumn**: Purge in the ranks of the Communist Party.

1922 **March 27–April 2**: Eleventh Communist Party Congress. **April 3**: Stalin is named Secretary General of the Communist Party. **April 10–May 19**: Conference of Genoa for economic recovery in Europe; participation of a Soviet delegation. **April 16**: Treaty of Rapallo with Germany. **May 25**: Lenin suffers a stroke. **June 9–August 9**: Socialist revolutionary trials. **November 4–December 5**: Fourth Komintern Congress. **December 16**: Lenin suffers a second stroke. **December 25**: Lenin's "Testament." **December 30**: Foundation of the USSR.

1923 **July 6**: A project for a Constitution is approved.

1924 **January 21**: Lenin dies. **January 31**: Ratification of the Constitution of the USSR.

Index of Names